the Best
SINGING GAMES
for children of all ages

By Edgar S. Bley

DRAWINGS BY PATT WILLEN

PIANO ARRANGEMENTS BY MARGARET CHASE

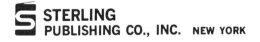
STERLING
PUBLISHING CO., INC. NEW YORK

Oak Tree Press Co., Ltd.
London & Sydney

CONTENTS

Fourteenth Printing, 1974

Copyright © 1957 by Sterling Publishing Co., Inc.
419 Park Avenue South, New York, N.Y. 10016
British edition published by Oak Tree Press Co., Ltd., Nassau, Bahamas
Distributed in Australia and New Zealand by Oak Tree Press Co., Ltd.,
P.O. Box 34, Brickfield Hill, Sydney 2000, N.S.W.
Distributed in the United Kingdom and elsewhere in the British Commonwealth
by Ward Lock Ltd., 116 Baker Street, London W 1
Manufactured in the United States of America
All rights reserved
Library of Congress Catalog Card No.: M 57-1014
ISBN 0-8069-4450-1   UK 7061-2232 1
4451-X

ACKNOWLEDGMENTS

Thanks to Mrs. Heman Chase of East Alstead, New Hampshire, for *Dollar, Dollar, The Miller Boy, Down the River* and *Pig in the Parlor,* all of which came out of her childhood in central Indiana. To William Sattler of New York City, who recalled *Send My Brown Jug Down to Town* and *Carousel* from his youth in Maryland. To Ruth and John J. Brooks of New York City for *Pass the Shoe,* which they learned in Georgia. And very special thanks to Elsa O. Bley, Alexandra Bley, Timothy Bley and Temma Bell for words, tunes and actions remembered—and for their willingness to be "borrowed" whenever I needed to reconstruct a motion or a step.

SONGS THAT PLAY GAMES

Songs and action are meant to go together. In the dim past, work songs evolved from the rhythm of labor, lullabies borrowed the beat of the mother's rocking arms. In the Old Testament, when music is mentioned, song and dance are referred to in the same breath. It is only in modern times, with grown-ups sitting motionless before the radio, phonograph or television set that song and action have become separate. And even now, if you look closely in the most respectable concert hall, you can often see the grown-up listener secretly tapping his foot in time . . .

This book is made up of singing games, action songs, "play parties," and other folk songs, all of which demand and produce related activity. Thus they are more than songs. They are songs and games in one or songs and dances combined. For children who think that they "don't like music," the actions distract them enough to let them sing with new pleasure and freedom.

FOR CHILDREN OF ALL AGES . . .

Music knows virtually no boundaries of age. Depending on the group of children you are working with—or on the momentary mood of the group—you will often amend the age levels indicated in this book or discard them entirely. Even the word *children* in the title is deceptive; the play parties suggested for more advanced fifth and sixth graders are no different from those played by teen-agers and adults in many rural areas. Try them yourself!

However, for convenience, the activities are marked for three age groups:

Preschool and *kindergarten* age: four-year-olds, five-year-olds and young sixes.
Primary grade level: ages 6, 7 and 8.
Elementary grade level: ages 9 through 12.

In the long run, parents and teachers and the children themselves will decide which of the games are right for them.

MUSICAL PLAY FOR PRESCHOOLERS . . .

For years and years, preschool children were limited to a diet of insipid music. It is only in recent years that we have learned—as our ancestors certainly must have known—that good robust folk music is fine fare for robust little children. They like it funny, they like it silly, they like it dramatic, they even like it pathetic. Story songs, like the *Cooper of Fife* or *Annie the Miller's Daughter,* can be shortened to one stanza. In all songs, little children should be encouraged to make up additional stanzas about the same topic or about themselves. Aside from singing and inventing new lyrics, activities at this age level involve pantomime or simple rhythmic play or a combination of both. Here again you can encourage the children's native creative ability.

SINGING GAMES FOR AGES 6 THROUGH 12 . . .

Some time late in the first grade or early in the second, on the average, children develop a great interest in highly organized group activities. They like situations where the rules are simple but firm. They like to know in advance exactly how things will work out. They like to have specific limits to their play areas. Thus singing games not only provide maximum physical activity in a limited space (a classroom or your living room on a rainy day), but they also provide a sense of "gathering together" following loose, wide-spread outdoor play like tag or hide-and-seek.

At this age children will still sometimes do free dramatization of songs, but they are most likely to do this in a very secure situation where they know each other very well and trust the adult in charge implicitly. Or they will prepare dramatizations of songs for performance. Otherwise they are prone to feel that such play is too young for them. At the other end of the scale, 7's and 8's who are good at singing games may well enjoy the simpler play parties. But the straight singing game, highly organized and not too "dancey," suits these youngsters best.

PLAY PARTIES FOR 9'S AND UP . . .

The play party is probably a native American invention. It is a combination of singing game and simple square dance. It differs from square dancing chiefly in that it needs neither musical instruments nor a caller. The players sing the music themselves and memorize the play patterns.

CHOOSING PARTNERS . . .

Little children will choose partners easily or accept partners with whom they are placed. However, there comes a time when boys and girls are embarrassed about picking partners or being picked. A good way to cope with this situation is to start your session with a game which does not require partners. Next play a game involving continual changing of partners. When this game ends, tell the children to remain with their partners of the moment and go immediately into a partnership game.

PROMENADE

In this step, boys have their partners on their right, unless otherwise specified, and all skip or shuffle counterclockwise. This puts the boys toward the center of the circle and the girls toward the outside. There are four ways of holding hands in the promenade. For the youngest children (or for a group going through the age of boy-girl diffidence) simply hold hands, boy's right and girl's left. The next stage is the "skaters' position" in which boy's right holds girl's right and boy's left holds girl's left, arms crossed in front. Two more graceful variants of this form are suitable for the oldest group. Both require left hands joined in front. In one, right hands are joined to the right of the girl's waist, with the boy's right arm passing behind her waist. In the other, right hands are joined near the girl's right shoulder, with the boy's right arm passing behind her shoulders.

BALANCE

Hop lightly on the left foot, swinging the right foot across in front of the left and back; then hop on right and swing the left across and back. For very young children, however, boys bow and girls curtsy.

GRAND RIGHT AND LEFT

Partners face each other, right hands joined. They walk past each other, holding out left hands to the next person, right to the following one, and so on. This causes all the boys to move around the circle to the right (counterclockwise) while all the girls move to the left (clockwise), and because they pass each other holding alternate hands, the boys' line and girls' line weave in and out of each other. In a set of four couples, original partners will end up together, but in the larger sets typical of singing games, this is a way of changing partners.

CORNER

This is a square dance term which is used here for convenience. It means the person beside you who is *not* your partner. A boy's corner is the girl on his left; a girl's corner is the boy on her right.

SWINGING

Swinging techniques must be developed gradually, as children grow. Preschool children, where swinging is called for, simply join right hands and skip around each other, although some people teach them to hook right elbows and skip around. The 6's through 8's will probably prefer the elbow swing. An alternative is to have them face each other, hold both hands and pivot.

Older children can be taught proper swinging. Thereafter they will use the elbow swing only when it is specifically called for. There are three factors in swinging:

1. Body position. Partners do not stand face to face, but side by side facing past each other. When they are thus placed, their feet will form a more-or-less straight line.

2. Hand position. Although many people hold each other as in ballroom dancing, the following holds are more suitable for children and in general more fun for everyone. Select *one* of the following, and stick to it. Place right hands on partners' right shoulders, and join left hands below. Or, place right

PROMENADE

GRAND RIGHT AND LEFT

SWINGING — BODY POSITION

SWINGING — HAND POSITION

hands on left side of partners' waists, with left hands joined below. Or, right hands behind right side of partners' waists, left hands joined below.

3. The step. Tiny hopping steps on right foot, and long pushing steps with the left. Left foot is always a little behind the right. It is something like riding a scooter, right foot on board and left foot behind and pushing—but don't forget the tiny little steps with the right foot or partners will trip each other as they go around.

ACCOMPANIMENT

The songs in this book have simple piano accompaniments. It is suggested that in playing, you keep them just that simple. Even better than the piano is a soft-spoken instrument that you hold in your hands, such as guitar, banjo, ukelele or autoharp; and best of all, as you gain confidence and skill, try doing without any instrument at all. The sooner your children and their friends (or your class, if you are a teacher) learn to sing and play these songs without accompaniment, the sooner they will be able to do them without you. Then in any appropriate situation, they will be ready for song and game without having to rely on grown-up supervision or support.

LONDON BRIDGE IS FALLING DOWN

Lon - don Bridge is fall - ing down,

fall-ing down, fall-ing down, Lon-don Bridge is

fall - ing down, My fair la - dy.

2
Build it up with sticks and stones, *etc.*

3
Sticks and stones will fall away, *etc.*

4
Build it up with iron bars, *etc.*

5
Iron bars will bend and break, *etc.*

6
Build it up with pins and needles, *etc.*

7
Pins and needles will rust and break, *etc.*

8
Take a key and lock her up, *etc.*

ACTION I (ages 4-5-6 and 7-8-9)

Two children join hands to make the bridge. The others form a single circle, passing under the bridge, and skip around the circle. At the end of each stanza, the children representing the bridge drop their hands and capture whoever is between them. They ask: "What will you pay? Silver or gold?" Before each stanza they have secretly agreed which one of them shall capture silver, which gold. The captured child responds, and he is told to stand behind the person whose metal he has guessed. When everyone has been captured, there will remain two lines, one behind each side of the bridge, each child holding on to the waist of the one in front. The game ends with a tug-of-war.

ACTION II (ages 7-8-9)

This game is played in couples. One couple forms the bridge, the others skip through holding hands or in promenade position. At the words, "My fair lady," the bridge couple drops its hands and captures the couple passing through. Then the last stanza is sung as a CHORUS, while the bridge couple sways from side to side, rocking the captured couple by doing so. At the end of the chorus, the captured couple becomes the bridge, while the former bridge rejoins the main circle of couples.

ACTION III (ages 4-5-6)

If you choose party refreshments with care, you can use this game to enable the children to set the table—a fine party activity. Have everything ready on a sideboard. Then sing, "Build it up with paper plates—with paper cups—with chocolate cupcakes—with lemonade." The children will pick up the tableware and food, carry it through the bridge and set it on the table. The last stanza might well be, "Find a chair and come and eat."

HERE WE GO ROUND THE MULBERRY BUSH

ACTION I (ages 4-5-6 and 7-8-9)

All over the United States this tends to be the favorite singing game for young children. Players form a circle, holding hands. As they sing Stanza 1, they circle to the left (clockwise). At the end of this stanza they drop hands, and in Stanzas 2 through 7 they act out the words of the song. There is no reason at all why their actions should be identical—better to have each youngster devise his own routine—but there is every reason why the actions should be done in time to the music. In Stanza 8 all skip counterclockwise, the girls holding out their skirts, the boys with a hand in a pocket, or any other hand-actions that they feel to be indicative of wearing one's best clothes.

ACTION II (ages 7-8-9)

For children who have outgrown this simplest form of action, there is an easy play party version of the game. Here the boys and girls are in couples. Stanza 1 is a promenade, not only at the beginning but as a chorus between every other stanza.

Each time the chorus ends, couples drop hands and face each other, the boys having their backs to the center of the circle, girls facing in, and pantomime the ensuing stanza. This position encourages some couples to work out the actions, such as *wringing* or *folding,* as a joint endeavor. After Stanza 7, players form promenade position but they sing Stanza 8 instead of the chorus. Instead of promenading around the circle, couples **now promenade** to their seats.

ACTION III (ages 7-8-9 and 10-11-12)

Here is a variation which brings about a change of partners after each promenade. While singing the words "in the morning," at the end of the chorus, couples drop hands, girls stop, and boys take one step backward. Thus, as the action stanza begins each boy is now facing a new partner (the girl who used to be behind him) and she remains his partner throughout this stanza and the promenade which follows.

HERE WE GO ROUND THE MULBERRY BUSH

1. Here we go round the mul-ber-ry bush, the mul-ber-ry bush, the mul-ber-ry bush.

Here we go round the mul-ber-ry bush, so ear-ly in the morn-ing.

2

This is the way we wash the clothes,
Wash the clothes, wash the clothes,
This is the way we wash the clothes,
So early Monday morning.

3

This is the way we wring the clothes, *etc.,*
So early Tuesday morning.

4

This is the way we hang the clothes, *etc.,*
So early Wednesday morning.

5

This is the way we sprinkle the clothes, *etc.,*
So early Thursday morning.

6

This is the way we iron the clothes, *etc.,*
So early Friday morning.

7

This is the way we fold the clothes, *etc.,*
So early Saturday morning.

8

This is the way we wear the clothes,
Going to church, going to church,
This is the way we wear the clothes,
So early Sunday Morning.

DOLLAR, DOLLAR

Indiana

Dol-lar, dol-lar, how you wan-der, from one hand in-to an-oth-er. Is it fair?

Is it fair? To keep that dol-lar hid-ing there?

ACTION (ages 7-8-9 and 10-11-12)

This is a circle game. All except one sit on the floor in a circle, facing in. Each child with his left hand grasps the right wrist of the person seated to his left. The person in the middle hands a button (representing a silver dollar) to a member of the circle. While the song is sung, those in the circle pass the "dollar" from right hand to right hand, in either direction. Those who do not have the "dollar" must also act as though they were passing it, and at the end of the song the person in the middle must guess who is holding it. If he succeeds he takes that person's place, while the one who held the "dollar"

goes to the middle. If he guesses wrong, he must remain in the center and try again.

It is generally a good idea to decide in advance that nobody may be It for more than two—or three—successive turns. If the limit is reached and he still has not guessed correctly, choose anyone who has not yet been in the middle to take his place.

The hand play of *Dollar, Dollar* is too difficult for children younger than six or seven, but there is no upper age limit to this game. For very young children, "Ring on a String" (on the next page) is a better possibility.

RING ON A STRING

"Let's go hunt-ing," says Risk-y Rob; "Let's go hunt-ing," says

Ben-nie to Bob, "Let's go hunt-ing," says Ja-cob to Joe,

"Hunt for a ring,"___ says Bil-ly Bar-low.

2
"What shall we hunt for," says Risky Rob,
"What shall we hunt for?" says Bennie to Bob,
"What shall we hunt for?" says Jacob to Joe,
"Ring on a string," says Billy Barlow.

3
"How shall we find it?" *etc.*
"Watch with a spy glass," says Billy Barlow.

4
"Where shall we find it?" *etc.*
"On somebody's finger," says Billy Barlow.

ACTION (all ages)

This game, like "Dollar, Dollar," is another singing version of "Button, Button, Who's Got the Button?" Take a length of string sufficient to pass comfortably through the hands of all those seated in the circle. Thread on a ring, and knot the string so as to make it into one continuous circle. The players all make passing motions, trying to conceal the whereabouts of the ring. At the end of each stanza, the child in the middle has to guess who has it. When he succeeds he joins the circle and is replaced by the person caught with the ring.

Even very young children can manage "Ring on a String," but it is suitable for all ages—and the players will go home humming the tune.

IN AND OUT THE WINDOW

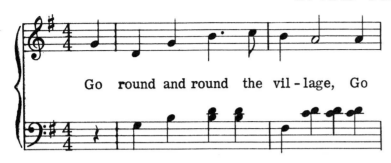

Go round and round the vil-lage, Go

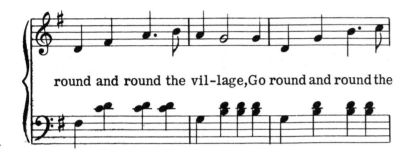

round and round the vil-lage, Go round and round the

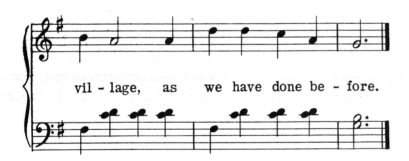

vil-lage, as we have done be-fore.

ACTION I (ages 4-5-6 and 7-8-9)

All players but one (It) stand in a circle, holding hands. It skips around the circle during Stanza 1. During Stanza 2, the children in the circle raise their hands and the odd one goes in one "window" and out the next, right around the circle or until the stanza ends. In Stanza 3, he takes a partner into the middle and they balance and swing. Stanzas 4 and 5 are like the first two, except that there are now two children skipping around together. During Stanza 6, It again skips around the outside of the circle alone, then takes his place as part of the circle at the end. The whole game starts again without pause, the partner now being It.

ACTION II (ages 7-8-9 and 10-11-12)

This version of the game is played entirely in couples. While singing Stanza 1, the first couple promenades outside the circle. Stanza 2, they promenade in and out of the "windows." The words of Stanza 3 are changed as follows:

> Now swing your partner, swing'er
> In the middle of the ring-a,
> And after you do swing 'er
> Go back and take your place.

For Stanza 4, all face to the right and walk in single file counterclockwise, each boy following his partner. Some people, for the last line of Stanza 4, substitute the words, "Next

2
Go in and out the window (3x)
As we have done before

3
Now go and pick a partner
Now balance to your partner
Now swing your brand-new partner
As we have done before

4
Now follow me to Boston (3x)
As we have done before

5
Go in and out the window (3x)
As we have done before

6
Now run and leave your partner (3x)
As we have done before

IN AND OUT THE WINDOW

couple ready to go." Since Stanzas 5 and 6 are omitted in this game, the song now starts again without pause, and the next couple to the right goes round and round the village.

ACTION III (ages 10-11-12)

This play party from Tennessee is for "experts." Children must be familiar with rather complex play parties or with square dancing before trying this one. It is played with four couples to a set. If you have eight or twelve couples, there can be several sets.

Stanza 1. First couple promenades once around couple II, ending up facing this couple, backs to couple IV.

Stanza 2. Couples I, II and IV all move forward. Couple I raises hands. Couple II ducks under the arms of couple I, then raises its arms for couple IV. Couple IV ducks under the arms of couple II, then raises its arms for couple I which has turned and is now returning. As each couple passes out of the set, it turns, still holding hands, so the boy continues to have his partner on his right, and starts back into the set without losing a step. There is just time for all three couples to return to place. This delightful figure is easier to do than to describe. There are two tricks to make it come out right: All three couples involved (couple III is idle throughout this stanza) move continually from the first note of the stanza to the last, alternately raising arms and ducking under. If you are in the middle, moving out of the set, hold your hands high; if you are on the outside, moving into the set, duck under. Memorize: *inside high, outside low*.

Stanza 4. First couple goes to third couple. All join right hands and walk clockwise, two complete turns. (This figure is sometimes called a right-hand star.)

Now sing Stanzas 1 and 2 again. Couple I goes to couple IV, promenades around them, and then in and out the window as before. The only difference between this action and the previous action for Stanza 2 is that the active couple starts out facing *couple IV* and moving in that direction. Couple III is again inactive.

Last stanza. Sing: "Now promenade your partner," etc.

The active couple has stepped into its own place and all four couples promenade once around the circle.

The above routine is repeated four times, with each couple in turn becoming the active couple. Note the order of stanzas: 1, 2, 4, 1, 2, promenade.

RIFLEMEN OF BENNINGTON

1. Why come ye hith - er red coats, your mind what mad-ness fills? In our val - leys there is

dan-ger and there's dan-ger in our hills. Oh,— hear ye not the sing-ing of the bu-gle wild and

free? And soon ye'll know the ring-ing of the ri-fle from the tree.

CHORUS

Oh, the ri - fle, (Clap, clap,

clap) Oh, the ri - fle, (Clap, clap, clap) In our hands will prove no tri -fle! (Clap, clap, clap)

RIFLEMEN OF BENNINGTON

ACTION (ages 7-8-9 and 10-11-12)

The Riflemen is a first-rate song in its own right to which the traditional hand actions add another dimension.

Here the three claps, representing the sound of rifle fire, must be absolutely precise. Their time value is three eighth notes, followed by an eighth rest. Discourage the group from doing any clapping during the rest of the song, since the contrast between the singing parts and the staccato claps provides musical interest.

You may do a soft marching rhythm with your feet while singing the verses but not during the chorus. Or you may pantomime the firing of a rifle at the appropriate moments in the chorus, the hands moving easily from this gesture to clapping.

2
Ye ride a goodly steed. Ye may know another master.
Ye forward come with speed but ye'll learn to go back faster.
Then ye'll meet our mountain boys and their leader, Johnny Stark,
Lads who make but little noise but who always hit their mark.

3
Tell him who stays at home, or across the briny water,
That hither he must come like bullock to the slaughter.
If we the work must do, why the sooner 'tis begun,
If flint and trigger hold but true the sooner 'twill be done.

THE INSTRUMENT SONG
Music on next two pages

ACTION (all ages)

The song leader, who is Father, starts each song with the question: "Children, guess what I have here?" The group responds, "Tell us, tell us, father dear." FATHER: "A fiddle fine I've brought today." CHILDREN: "Show us how to make it play." FATHER: (sings and pantomimes the violin) "Shusti, fiddli, fiddli, shusti, fiddli, fiddli, that's how the fiddle plays." CHILDREN: (imitating gestures as well as words) "Shusti, fiddli, fiddli, shusti, fiddli, fiddli, that's how it plays."

After the second stanza, the *doodli, doodli, opp* section is immediately followed by the entire *shusti, fiddli, fiddli* section, both father's and children's parts. This is continued, so that the last stanza ends with the singing and playing of all the instruments in reverse order, ending as each stanza does with *shusti, fiddli, fiddli,* that's how it plays.

The play acting is the closest pantomime you can devise. the bass drum stanza has an unexpected set of gestures, however. The drum is supposed to be worked by a foot pedal, so that at the word *Boom* each person stamps his right foot on the floor. At *chin-da* each person claps twice, with the hands moved vertically and clapping as they pass, as cymbals are played. Thus, this stanza differs from the others in having sounds (*stamp, clap, clap, stamp, clap, clap*) as well as gestures added to the singing.

Once children are familiar with this song, you can give a child the opportunity of being the father. Or let a different child be father for each stanza. Some groups will wish to add more instruments, making up funny but appropriate sounds and suitable gestures. However this song is sung and played, one thing is important. The voice should imitate the quality of the particular instrument, brassy and hard for the trumpet, tinkling for the harp, and so on. This is half the fun, and the groups who sing it best will enjoy it most.

THE INSTRUMENT SONG

Chil - dren guess what I have here? Show us, show us, fa - ther dear

1. A fid - dle fine I've brought to - day.___ Show us how to make it play.___
2. A clar - i - net with sil - ver on it Show us how to play up - on it.
3. A trum - pet fine for you to blow___ Show us how to make it go.___
4. A big bass viol I've brought for you___ Show us how to play it, too.___
5. A gold - en harp with col - ored strings_ Show us fa - ther how it rings.___
6. A big bass drum with cym - bals round___ Show us how to make them sound.___

1. through 5.   D.C.

1. Shus-ti, fid-dli, fid-dli, That's how the fid-dle plays. Shus-ti, fid-dli, fid-dli, That's how it plays.___

6.   Fine

That's how they play.___ 2. Doo-dli, doo-dli, opp, That's how the clar-i-net plays, Doo-dli, doo-dli, opp,

THE INSTRUMENT SONG

That's how it plays._(to Shusti) 3. Ta-ta-ra, That's how the trum-pet plays, Ta-ta-ra, That's how it

plays. (to Doodli) 4. Brum, fritz, fritz, That's how the bass viol plays, Brum, fritz, fritz, That's how it plays. (to Ta-ta-ra)

5. Brink-i, sfink-i, sfink-i, That's how the harp plays, Brink-i, sfink-i, sfink-i, That's how it plays. (to Brum)

6. Boom, chin-da, That's how the bass drum plays, Boom, chin-da, That's how it plays. (to Brinki)

ANNIE THE MILLER'S DAUGHTER

ACTION I (ages 7-8-9 and 10-11-12)

Annie is another fine song which is improved when punctuated with claps by the singers. While teaching the song, play a thumping accompaniment in the clapping measures; but when the children have mastered it, use no accompaniment during the claps at all. In this way you will stress the contrast between singing and clapping. Encourage singers to devise rhythms for clapping, by inviting a volunteer to set a pattern in advance, with the understanding that all will follow his pattern and that another child will set the rhythm another time. Aside from the four quarter notes shown, here are two good patterns:

ACTION II (ages 7-8-9 and 10-11-12)

This song, like many humorous ballads, is excellent for acting out, either impromptu or rehearsed. We saw ten children play it, with one being Annie, one being the Faithful Lover, and the rest being geese. During the first line Annie minced around the room, followed by the geese who imitated and exaggerated her gait. The geese clapped by holding their hands in front of their faces as beaks. During the second line, the geese waddled off, during the third line they swam an imaginary stream, and during the fourth they squatted on the other side while Annie looked at them and pantomimed despair.

The first two lines of Stanza 2 were devoted to exaggerated heroics on the part of the Faithful Lover. Instead of clapping, he stamped his feet impressively. During the third line he swam the river and chased the geese back across. During the fourth line he swam back and wrung out his clothing.

In Stanza 3 there was exaggerated pantomime of courtship, with the geese watching and clapping. During the last chorus line the geese closed in around Annie and the Faithful Lover, flapping their wings and concealing them from the audience, to provide a fine finale.

ACTION III (ages 4-5-6)

This song can be used with very young children by eliminating Stanzas 2 and 3. The melody will delight them, and there are enough possibilities for dramatic play in the first stanza alone.

ANNIE THE MILLER'S DAUGHTER

1. An - nie the mil - ler's daugh-ter, walk - ing be-side the wa - ter, An - nie, An - nie!

(clap, clap, clap, clap) Far off your flock has wan - dered, While you have strolled and pon-dered,

An - nie, An - nie! (clap, clap, clap, clap) O'er the mill - stream they me-an - der Oh dear, oh dear!
Ev'-ry goose and ev'-ry gan-der Oh dear, oh dear!

2
Annie, your faithful lover soon will your flock recover,
   Annie, Annie! (Clap, clap, clap, clap.)
"I'll swim the rushing river, yes, for your sake I'll shiver,
   "Annie, Annie! (Clap, clap, clap, clap!)
"Chilly water I am loathing, oh dear, oh dear!
"Dripping wet my Sunday clothing, oh dear, oh dear!"

3
"Now with your flock before you, proving that I adore you,
   "Annie, Annie! (Clap, clap, clap, clap.)
"No longer let us tarry, tell me when we shall marry,
   "Annie, Annie! (Clap, clap, clap, clap.)
"Do not let me drown in sorrow, oh dear, oh dear!
"Say you'll marry me tomorrow, my dear, so dear!"

BLUEBELL, BLUEBELL

Blue - bell, blue - bell, through my win - dow, Blue - bell, blue - bell,

through my win - dow, Blue - bell, blue - bell, through my win - dow;

Oh, John - nie I am tir - ed.

BLUEBELL, BLUEBELL

ACTION I (ages 4-5-6 and 7-8-9)

This is a simple circle game. All stand in a circle, holding hands. One person is It. He weaves in and out of the circle until the last line, at which time he stands, drooping, in front of another child. Then the Johnnie in front of whom he is standing becomes It, while the tired one becomes a member of the circle.

ACTION II (ages 4-5-6)

Bluebell, Bluebell lends itself to free play, with children having the choice between acting the people who are looking at the bluebells and acting the part of the flowers. New words are especially easy to create: "Oh, Johnnie, I am hungry," at lunch time, or, "Oh, Johnnie, put your coat on," when it is time to go out.

ACTION III (ages 10-11-12)

For older children there is a very graceful play party to the same song. There must be an even number of couples, preferably at least six, with no upper limit except what the room will hold. Have the couples count off, *one, two, one, two,* etc. All the *one* couples face counterclockwise, the boy being toward the center of the circle, the girl toward the outside. All the *two* couples face clockwise, the boy being on the outside of the circle and the girl inside. Couples hold hands.

All walk forward in time to the music, alternately raising hands over the approaching couple and ducking under the hands of the next couple. Always start each stanza with the *number one* couples having hands raised high, the *number twos* ducking through the window. Once in each measure, every couple passes over or under another couple. Stop at the end of the third line of the song.

During the fourth line, each girl steps forward toward the girl opposite her, holding out right hand. They clasp right hands briefly, while passing each other. As they pass, each one holds out her left hand toward the opposite boy who takes it with his left hand. (At this point, the two girls have exchanged partners.) The boy executes an about-face to the left, still holding left hands, and puts his right arm around the girl's waist. For a moment each girl leans on her new partner's arm, in pantomime of being tired. They then drop left hands, and the boy drops his hand from the girl's waist, and they join hands as in the beginning, boy's right holding girl's left, ready to start the next stanza.

During the fourth line in this figure two things have happened. Each girl has exchanged partners, *number one* girls moving to the next boy counterclockwise, *number two* girls moving to the next boy clockwise. And each boy has changed his direction, *number ones* becoming *twos* and vice versa. This is important to remember, since the *ones* always start the stanza with arms raised, and the *twos* always start by ducking. The trick is that as each stanza begins, the girls give their partners the clue, since girls do not change number throughout the game.

FOUR IN A BOAT

ACTION I (ages 7-8-9 and 10-11-12)

All players except four boys form a circle, facing in and holding hands. They move to the left (clockwise) throughout Stanzas 1 and 2. The four boys form a circle in the middle, holding hands and facing out. During the first three lines of Stanza 1, they move to their left (counterclockwise). At the last line of the stanza, each boy takes a partner from the outer circle and brings her into the center.

During Stanza 2, the boys in the boat put their partners on their right and all eight join hands and turn counterclockwise, as before.

In Stanza 3, both circles stop turning. The boys in the boat swing their partners. In Stanza 4, the middle circle is reformed and both circles turn in opposite directions. While the last line is sung, with both circles still turning, the boys in the boat leave their partners and rejoin the outer circle.

The game starts again immediately, with the girls in the boat. This time sing "sailor boy" instead of "pretty gal."

ACTION II (ages 10-11-12)

A variation on this play party is used on the Kentucky side of the Ohio River. In this form, the four boys in the middle form a star, each having his left arm extended toward the center, the four left hands joined and the boys walking counterclockwise. (A good way to join hands in this and other star formations is for each person to grasp the wrist of the person in front of him.) The outer circle moves clockwise.

When the boys take partners at the end of Stanza 1, they do so without breaking their star. Each boy puts his right arm around the waist of his partner, the boys' left hands still being joined in the middle, thus forming what is known as a gents' grand star. Each couple is now like a spoke in a wheel, the boys' left hands making the hub, and the boat turns counterclockwise for Stanza 2. Break and swing for Stanza 3, but as Stanza 4 begins, reform the grand star.

At the words "swing her in" in the last line of Stanza 4, the boys drop left hands and each couple pivots so that the girls are in the middle. Girls join right hands, and they and their partners walk clockwise, forming a ladies' grand star. At the last word in the song, the boys drop their arms from their partners' waists and rejoin the circle, leaving the girls in star formation ready to start the game over again.

Note that in the second round, and every round starting with *girls* in the boat, the big circle turns to the right (counterclockwise). And, of course, everyone sings "get me a sailor boy," instead of "pretty gal."

FOUR IN A BOAT

Four in a boat and the waves run high, Four in a boat and the waves run high,

Four in a boat and the waves run high, Get me a {pret-ty gal / sail-or boy

Repeat | Last time

bye and bye. | bye and bye.

2
Get me a pretty gal (sailor boy), stay all day (3x)
We don't care what the teachers say.

3
Eight in the boat and it won't go 'round (3x)
Swing the pretty gal (sailor boy) you've just found.

4
Eight in the boat and it goes once more (3x)
Swing her (him) in and swim for shore.

ACTION III (ages 4-5-6 and 7-8-9)

Small children like the tune and the simple, repetitious words. Use it for free rhythmic play based on rowing or rolling. Or make a singing game based on the rowing game that children play in twos, sitting opposite each other on the floor, hands joined, and alternately leaning forward and lying back.

Start with "two in a boat," the others sitting around in a circle. For the fourth line, substitute "get me a partner" for the "pretty gal." At the end of the stanza, have each one pick a partner, making two pairs in the middle, and sing "four in a boat." When these children pick partners, sing "eight in a boat" and eventually "16" and "32" if you have children enough and space enough. Use only Stanza 1 with the suggested numerical changes.

23

THE COOPER OF FIFE

ACTION (all ages)

This song is commonly used for play acting. First teach the song whole, explaining the difficult words and ideas. "Gentle" here means upper class, not kindly. The barrelmaker has married an upper class woman who won't do her work, but he cannot beat her for fear of the reprisal of her aristocratic relatives. "Cairding" is carding the wool. "Gouden" is golden. The last stanza is rather enigmatic, for children, and you had better explain that the moral of the song is simply this: If your wife thinks she is too good to do her share of the work, it is up to you to make her.

Next, have the whole group sing while two members act out the part of cooper and wife. Or play it with three soloists: a narrator to sing the solo parts of Stanzas 1 through 5 and Stanza 10, the cooper to sing Stanza 6, and a wife to sing Stanzas 7, 8 and 9. The rest of the group sings the chorus lines throughout. Some of the actions will take longer than the verses allow, and for these you can play the melody several times through on the piano, without any singing, or the chorus can hum or whistle the tune.

This sort of comic ballad should always be acted broadly, with a great deal of exaggeration. However, remind the actors that whatever else they do, they should keep in time to the music. The chorus, too, has acting as part of its responsibility. Like the chorus in the Greek drama, these children represent the villagers who react to the story as it unfolds. In the first stanza they laugh at the cooper. In the second through fourth they show their disapproval of the wife. In the fifth they portray wonder. In Stanza 6 horror during the first line changes to amusement in the second line. During the seventh, eighth, and ninth stanzas, they nod approvingly at the wife's reformed behavior. In the last, they show their admiration for the cooper who has tricked the aristocrats.

ACTION (ages 4-5-6)

For children too young to learn the words of the verses, the adult can sing while the children freely pantomime the actions. (The chorus should present no difficulties, as children love nonsense syllables.) Let the children act out any roles they prefer—it doesn't matter if there are a dozen wives or a dozen coopers.

ACTION (ages 10-11-12)

The addition of properties and costumes for this age group will enhance the fun. They can be impromptu and simple, or elaborate enough to convert this into a stage presentation.

2
She wadna caird, she wadna spin,
For shamin' o' her gentle kin.
3
She wadna bake, she wadna brew,
For spilin' o' her comely hue.
4
She wadna wash, she wadna wring,
For losin' o' her gouden ring.
5
The cooper is gone to his woo' shack,
And laid a sheepskin across his wife's back.
6
"I wadna thrash ye, for your gentle kin,
"But I will thrash me ain sheepskin!"
7
"Oh, I will caird, an' I will spin,
"An' think nae mair o' me gentle kin."
8
"An' I will bake, an' I will brew,
"An' think nae mair o' me comely hue."
9
"Oh, I will wash, an' I will wring,
"An' think nae mair o' me gouden ring."
10
All ye wha ha' gotten a gentle wife,
Just send ye for the wee cooper o' Fife.

THE COOPER OF FIFE

There was a wee coop-er who lived__ in Fife. Nick-e-ty, nock-e-ty, noo, noo, noo; And he had mar-ried a gen-tle wife, Hey, Wil-ly Wol-lack-y, ho, John Dou-gal, A - lain Qua-roosh-i-ty, roo, roo, roo.

SOLO: There was a wee cooper who lived in Fife,
   CHORUS: Nickety, nackety, noo, noo, noo,

SOLO: And he had married a gentle wife,
   CHORUS: Hey, Willy Wollacky, ho, John Dougal,
      Alain Quarooshity, roo, roo, roo.

25

OLD WOMAN

ACTION I (all ages)

Dramatic singing: The boys **ask the** questions, singing very loudly in Stanzas 1 through 4. The fifth stanza they sing much more softly, and the sixth they whisper as quietly as they can without losing the melody. The girls sing the answers, emphasizing the word *speak* in a loud, rather squeaky voice. In the fifth stanza they should sing it still more loudly, and the *laws-a-mercy* of the last stanza should be almost shouted.

ACTION II (ages 4-5-6 and 7-8-9)

Singing and pantomime: The group sings the song dramatically, as above, while one boy and one girl play the parts. You will find that once you have done it this way, children will ask for it again and again. For a performance you will need hill billy props—corncob pipes, earthenware jug, an imitation chicken or lamb for Stanza 4, and suitable costumes including bare feet, and whiskers for the old man.

ACTION III (ages 10-11-12)

In the Great Smokies there is a play party version of Old Woman. Any number of couples form a ring, girls on the boys' right. While the boys sing the questions, in every stanza, all promenade. It is necessary to use that promenading position in which the boy's right arm crosses behind the girl's shoulders and they clasp right hands at her right shoulder. Left hands may be joined in front, or may be left free to pantomime the words of the song.

Stanzas 1 through 4: Promenade during the question. On the word *speak*, girls stamp a foot, do a left-about-face under the boys arm and promenade in the opposite direction. (At this point, the boys are promenading in the usual direction, counterclockwise, and the girls in the reverse direction.) At the repeat of **the** word *speak*, girls again stamp a foot and

everyone about-faces and continues the promenade. (Now the girls are going counterclockwise and the boys clockwise.) As each stanza ends, partners will be reunited, ready for the next promenade.

Stanza 5: Promenade. At the word *speak*, the girl turns under the boy's arm, but they do not drop right hands. She walks two steps back, right about face, and returns to his side in two steps, again passing under his arm. Repeat.

Stanza 6: Promenade. During the answer, partners join right elbows and swing, stamping their feet in time as they turn, until the end of the game.

OLD WOMAN

Old wo - man, old wo - man, are you fond of walk - ing?

Speak a lit - tle loud - er, sir, I'm ra - ther hard of hear - ing.

2
Old woman, old woman, are you fond of smoking? (2x)
Speak a little louder, sir, I'm rather hard of hearing. (2x)

3
Old woman, old woman, are you fond of drinking? (2x)
Speak a little louder, sir, I'm rather hard of hearing. (2x)

4
Old woman, old woman, are you fond of eating? (2x)
Speak a little louder, sir, I'm rather hard of hearing. (2x)

5
Old woman, old woman, are you fond of courtin'? (2x)
Speak a little louder, sir, I just begin to hear you! (2x)

6
Old woman, old woman, will you come and marry me? (2x)
LAWS-A-MERCY on my soul, but now I really hear you! (2x)

27

BUFFALO GALS

Traditional: Oh, Buf-fa-lo gals won't you come out to - night, won't you come out to - night, won't you
Play Party: 1. First Buf-fa-lo boy go___ round the out - side, go___ round the out - side, go___

come out to - night? Oh, Buf-fa-lo gals won't you come out to - night and
round the out - side, First Buf-fa-lo boy go_____ round the out - side, and

CHORUS

dance by the light of the moon._____ Oh,
bal - ance___ to your___ cor - ner. O h, (Chorus I:) turn your part-ner with a

right hand round, and your cor - ner la - dy with a left hand round, Oh you

swing your part - ner off the ground, Prom-en - ade by the light of the moon.

CHORUS II

Will you, won't you, will you, won't you, come out tonight,
Won't you come out tonight, won't you come out tonight?
Oh, will you, won't you, will you, won't you come out tonight,
Promenade by the light of the moon.

2
Two Buffalo Boys go round the outside, *etc.*

3
Three Buffalo Boys go round the outside, *etc.*

4
Four Buffalo Boys go round the outside, *etc.*

ACTION I (ages 4-5-6)

Buffalo Gals (Buffalo Boys) is a natural for the very young. The rhythm demands dancing and the words are sure to intrigue. This can be a circle game or it can be dramatic play, with the girls in a corner or in the next room until the chorus. This song is good for individual dancing, too.

Have all in a circle. The leader calls out the name of one of the children as the group sings "Buffalo gals," and that child dances in the center. The solo may continue through the chorus, or the chorus may be an occasion for the others to dance, approximating the actions originated by the soloist.

ACTION II (ages 7-8-9 and 10-11-12)

This play party is really like an easy square dance with the calls sung by the dancers themselves. It requires four couples to a set.

The first couple is usually the couple with its back to the music, but if you are using no accompaniment, designate a first couple in each set. The boy in the first couple shuffles all around the outside of the set, clockwise, back to his own place where he balances to his corner. Now sing the chorus melody to the first set of words while everyone turns first his partner, then his corner, and all couples swing during the last two lines. The fourth line, with the instruction to promenade, is an advance warning. Swing until the end of that line, but be ready to start the promenade on the first words of Chorus II. Promenade two complete circles during Chorus II.

In Stanza 2, the head boy is followed by the boy in couple II. In Stanza 3, he is followed by the second and third boys.

In Stanza 4, all the boys go around. Always sing both choruses after every stanza. After the fourth stanza and chorus, you can begin all over with, "First Buffalo Gal go round the outside." Continue through four stanzas with the girls active. The girls go around the set counterclockwise.

ACTION III (ages 10-11-12)

This play party uses the traditional words given with the music. It requires sets of four couples each.

Verse figure: ladies' grand chain. The four girls step forward with right hands extended. Join four right hands, like the spokes of a wheel, and turn the wheel clockwise half a revolution.

Girls hold out left hands to the boys who were originally across the set from them. Boys take girls' left hands in their own left hands; put right hands on the girls' waists and turn them, boys stepping back in place, girls forward. (At the end of the line two, all are standing in couples, girls on the boys' right, but the girls are across the set from their starting places.)

Without pausing, the girls step forward with right hands extended again, and turn the wheel an additional three-quarters of a revolution—that is, until they have gone one place further than back to their original partner. Left hand to *new* partner who takes it in his left hand and turns her. (At the end of the verse, positions are similar to those at the beginning of the game, except that each girl has moved one place to the left. When verse and chorus have been sung four times, each girl will end up with her original partner.

Chorus figure: allemande left, followed by grand right and left. The allemande left is performed by having corners join left hands and walk around each other, once, back to place. This leaves each person facing his partner with right hands ready to begin the grand right and left. (This sequence—allemande left followed by grand right and left—is found in many of the more complicated play parties and in at least half the common square dances. However, it is best not to teach it until a group has thoroughly mastered the unadorned grand right and left.)

The verse follows the chorus without pause. In fact, through the entire four verses and four choruses of this game the girls move continuously, never missing a step.

WHEN I WAS SINGLE

ACTION I (ages 4-5-6)

Although the words seem a little sophisticated for them, small children like both melody and lyrics of this song. A very simple version of the singing game is suitable for this age group. All form a ring around one boy in the middle.

Stanza 1: The circle skips to the left, the husband in the opposite direction.

Stanza 2: The husband picks a partner and skips to the right with her, while the circle continues skipping to the left.

Stanza 3: The circle stands still, clapping and singing, while the pair in the middle play out the action.

Stanza 4: The husband picks a new partner, skips with her to the right, while the circle resumes its skipping to the left.

Start over again with the second wife as the person in the middle; change the words to "I married a husband," etc. At the end of this round, the second husband will remain to be soloist in the third round, with the original words.

ACTION II (ages 7-8-9 and 10-11-12)

Players form a ring, facing left, except for one boy in the middle. Stanza 1 is sung at a lively pace. The circle skips merrily, clockwise, while the boy in the center skips counterclockwise.

Stanza 2 should be sung a bit more slowly and deliberately. The boy in the center picks a partner. For the first two lines, the circle marches clockwise, while the couple in the center marches in the reverse direction, side by side, as though at a wedding. During the second two lines, the outer circle stops. The husband drops the wife's hand and puts his hands over his ears, skipping ahead of her. She follows with pantomime of scolding.

Stanza 3 is sung very slowly and solemnly until the word *laughed*, at which point it returns to the original skipping tempo. The circle stands still and watches, during the first 2½ lines, while the wife lies down and dies. In fact, she generally dies three times, sitting up on the *oh thens* and dying again when the words indicate. At the word *laugh* the husband skips around the "dead" wife while the onlookers skip around the circle.

The tempo of Stanza 4, like that of Stanza 2, is stately. The boy picks a new wife and marches with her around the "dead" one, the circle marching clockwise. As the last two lines are sung, the circle stands still, watching. The husband runs around with his hands over his head while the new wife chases him, pantomiming action with an imaginary rolling pin. At the last minute, the boy and both partners rejoin the circle, the boy designating a new husband to step into the middle as the whole game begins again.

ACTION III (ages 10-11-12)

As a play party, *I Wish I Was Single* works with any number of couples, preferably six or more. Stanza 1 is a grand right and left. As Stanza 2 begins, each boy takes the girl he is now abreast of, and all promenade. Pantomime during the last two lines is suitable, but do not allow it to break the rhythm or formation of the promenade.

Stanza 3: The wife "dies" in the first line, "recovers" in the second line, "dies for good" in the third, as follows: Couples stop, facing each other, boys having their backs to the inside of the circle. They are still holding hands from the promenade, right hand in right, left in left. Boys step forward on right foot, girls back on left sinking down to the ground. Boys back on right, pulling girls up again. Repeat first action, thus leaving all the girls lying on their backs, feet toward the center of the circle. During the last line, boys move counterclockwise inside the circle of girls' feet.

Stanza 4: Each boy takes as his second wife the girl he is abreast of when this stanza begins. Promenade to end of song and start Stanza 1 again without pause.

WHEN I WAS SINGLE

When I was sin-gle, oh then, oh then, when I was sin-gle, oh then,____ When I was sin-gle my pock-ets did jin-gle, and I wish I was sin-gle a- gain, a-gain, and I wish I was sin-gle a - gain.____

2
I married a wife, oh then, oh then,
I married a wife, oh then,
I married a wife, she's the plague o' my life,
And I wish I was single again, again, and I wish I was single again.

3
My wife she died, oh then, oh then,
My wife she died, oh then,

My wife she died and I laughed til I cried,
To think I was single again, again, to think I was single again.

4
I married another, oh then, oh then,
I married another, oh then,
I married another, the devil's grandmother,
And I wish I was single again, again, and I wish I was single again.

JOHN BROWN'S BABY

John Brown's ba - by had a cold up - on his chest, John Brown's

ba - by had a cold up - on his chest, John Brown's ba - by had a

cold up - on his chest, And they rubbed it with cam - phor - a - ted oil.

ACTION (all ages)

This old favorite is not only fun, but a fine exercise for developing accurate timing. First sing the song through as it stands. Next, sing it omitting the word *baby*, each time it occurs, and substituting a pantomime of rocking a baby in one's arms. The next time, continue to rock the baby instead of singing the word, and in addition substitute the sound of a cough for the word *cold*. The next round, remove the word *chest*, in addition to the others, and substitute a rap on your own chest. In the following round, use pantomime in place of singing the word *rubbed*. Finally you pantomime camphorated oil, which has an unpleasant odor, by holding your nose.

The important part to remember is that wherever you leave out a word you must allow exactly the same amount of time as it would take if you were singing it. The final stanza sounds like this:

John Brown's (*rocking*) had a (*coughing*) upon his (*tapping*)

John Brown's (*rocking*) had a (*coughing*) upon his (*tapping*)

John Brown's (*rocking*) had a (*coughing*) upon his (*tapping*)

And they (*rubbing*) it with (*holding the nose*)

32

DID YOU EVER SEE A LASSIE?

Did you ev - er see a las - sie, a las - sie, a las - sie, Did you

ev - er see a las - sie go this way and that? Go this way and that way and

this way and that way, Did you ev - er see a las - sie go this way and that?

ACTION (ages 4-5-6 and 7-8-9)

All children but one form a circle, holding hands. One child is in the middle. If the leader is a girl, sing the song as written above. When a boy is in the middle, sing, "Did you ever see a *laddie?*"

The children forming the circle skip clockwise. The leader plans some kind of action, which he performs at the words *this way and that*. The circle stops moving and drops hands, and during the third and fourth lines all the children copy the action initiated by the leader.

Just as the song ends, the leader chooses another child to be the next leader. Then he steps back into the circle, taking the place of the child thus displaced.

The best actions are those which provide a contrast (such as hop left, hop right) and which can follow the rhythm of the song exactly.

HAPPY IS THE MILLER

ACTION I (ages 7-8-9 and 10-11-12)

Any number of couples form a circle, boys having partners on their right. Promenade from the beginning of the tune until the next-to-last measure. On the words *fall back,* boys release their partners and take one backward step while the girls continue one step forward. As the verse begins again each boy is abreast of the girl who was previously behind him. With new partners, the promenade begins again. Sing the verse through as many times as the number of couples you have in the set, and all will end up with their original partners.

If the set is not too big (four to eight couples), the boys may join left hands in the middle, holding their partners by right hands around the waist. In this way, the whole set becomes a gigantic wheel. Have each boy hold the wrist of the boy in front of him to form a secure and comfortable hub, and this grip should not be released throughout the dance, even though the boys disengage their *right* hands to change partners at the end of each verse.

In some communities the boy is allowed, if he has the courage, to kiss his partner at the words *takes his toll.*

ACTION II (ages 10-11-12)

This variant of the play party is somewhat more demanding. On the first line, promenade with boys holding left hands in the center. At the words *And he takes,* boys drop left hands and each couple pivots (boys stepping back, girls forward) so that the girls are now on the inside of the circle and the boys on the outside. The girls now join their right hands in the center, and the promenade continues in the opposite direction, clockwise. The change of direction is phrased by square dance callers as "ladies swing in, gents swing out," and it takes place in two measures of the music. This leaves only two more measures of the second line for the reverse promenade.

During the third line, there is an allemande left with the corner. That is, each boy joins left hands with the girl on his left and they walk around each other back to place.

The last line is the same as the first, promenade with boys' hands joined in the center, except that on the last measure the boys step backward while the girls move forward, so all end with new partners.

This play party is difficult not because it includes any complicated steps, but because it requires such fast changes. In teaching it, you might show the group how the song breaks down:

> Promenade, boys' hands joined—4 steps
> Girls swing in—2 steps
> Promenade, girls' hands joined—2 steps
> Allemande left—4 steps.
> Promenade, boys' hands joined—3 steps
> Girls forward, boys backward—1 step.

The mere knowledge that precision is demanded often makes it possible for people to produce it.

HAPPY IS THE MILLER

Oh,— hap-py is the mil-ler boy who lives in the mill, And he takes his

toll— with a right good will, One— hand on the hop-per and the oth-er in the

sack, And the wheel rolls— for-ward and the boys fall back.

SHE'LL BE COMING ROUND THE MOUNTAIN

She'll be com - ing round the moun - tain when she comes, (Toot, toot!) She'll be

com - ing round the moun - tain when she comes, (Toot, toot!) She'll be com - ing round the

moun - tain, she'll be com - ing round the moun - tain, She'll be com - ing round the

moun - tain when she comes! (Toot, toot!)

SHE'LL BE COMING ROUND THE MOUNTAIN

2

She'll be driving six white horses, when she comes, (*Whoa, back!*)

3

Oh, we'll all go out to meet her, when she comes, (*Hi, babe!*)

4

Oh, we'll kill the old red rooster, when she comes, (*Cockadoodle-doo!*)

5

And we'll all have chicken and dumplings, when she comes, (*Yum, yum!*)

6

Oh, she'll have to sleep with grandmaw, when she comes, (*Snore, snore!*)

7

And she'll wear red flannel pyjamas, when she comes, (*Wheee-whooo! snore, snore! yum, yum! cockadoodle-doo! hi, babe! whoa, back! toot, toot!*)

ACTION I (all ages)

The spoken words are cumulative at the end of each stanza (but not after the first and second lines of each stanza). Thus, Stanza 2 ends: "She'll be driving six white horses, when she comes, (*Whoa, back! toot, toot!*)" Each stanza adds one more until the final stanza ends as shown above.

Toot, toot is accompanied by two gestures of pulling the whistle cord in a locomotive. *Whoa, back* is accompanied by a long hard pull on the reins. *Hi, babe* demands a carefree flourish of the hand, in greeting. With *cockadoodle-doo* goes a flapping of the wings. *Yum, yum* is naturally accompanied by a rubbing of the stomach. The snores should be snoring *sounds*, but they should be in time, two staccato quarter notes with the accent on the second. No action is called for. In Stanza 7, the words printed above refer to a double whistle. The boys join thumbs and forefingers, and hold their hands to their eyes as though they were spectacles; the girls rise and graciously bow, as though in response to applause.

At the end of each stanza, while going through the different calls, make sure that each is accompanied by its appropriate gesture.

This game is a guaranteed ice-breaker for a group which has never done singing games together before.

ACTION II (ages 4-5-6)

Either with or without the repeated sounds at the ends of the lines, this song can be acted out time and again. If you have a large group, children can represent not only "she" and "we" and "grandmaw," but also the train, the horses, and the rooster.

Children naturally make up new words to this, once they have learned it well. "Oh, we all put on our raincoats when it rains, when it rains." "Oh, we put away our blocks before we eat, before we eat." And a thousand more!

PICK A BALE OF COTTON

ACTION I (ages 4-5-6 and 7-8-9)

This is a lively, robust song whose words and melody call for action. Be sure to contrast the long, loud notes of *Oh, Lordy* with the quick, rather quiet notes of the rest of the song.

Young children will work out for themselves actions to suit the words. Generally, during the words *Oh, Lordy* they stretch arms out and up in one long motion to contrast with the quick repeated motions of jumping, turning, and picking. With encouragement, children will invent new stanzas galore. This song is especially useful to accompany chores such as picking up toys, clearing a table, dressing or undressing, bathing or getting dried.

ACTION II (ages 10-11-12)

As a singing game, omit Stanzas 5 and 6. Start with the chorus. All form a circle, not holding hands. Choose one person for the first cotton picker.

Chorus: On *Oh, Lordy,* step to the left on the right foot, crossing it in front of the left; then step left on the left foot, then a short left step on the right, bring feet together. For *pick a bale of cotton,* pantomime bending to pick up a heavy sack in both hands and swinging it over right shoulder. On the second *Oh, Lordy,* step right on left foot, crossing it in front of the right. Right on right, then short right on left. For *pick a bale a day,* repeat the pantomime of lifting the sack. The entire figure is done twice.

Stanza 1: The selected cotton picker jumps into the middle of the circle, turns around, and "picks a bale o' cotton." This is done four times while the members of the circle watch.

Chorus: Circle dances same steps as before. Cotton picker does the same, solo, in the middle.

Stanza 2: Cotton picker chooses a partner who joins him in the middle. They face each other, jump up and land in a crouching position, hook right elbows and turn each other (the elbow swing) with knees deeply bent. Jump and swing four times.

Chorus: Same as before. Cotton picker and partner stand back to back in the middle, and do the same actions as the circle.

Stanza 3: Each of the two in the middle picks a new partner, and both couples repeat the action of Stanza 2, four times.

Chorus: The four in the center form a small circle, facing out, and perform the chorus steps, while those in the big circle again do it, facing in.

Stanza 4: The four in the middle march counterclockwise during the first line, clockwise on the second, counter on the third, and clockwise on the last. The big circle always marches in the opposite direction, thus starting to the left. As this stanza ends, the four in the middle rejoin the big circle, the original cotton picker choosing a new one to start the game again after the final chorus.

PICK A BALE OF COTTON

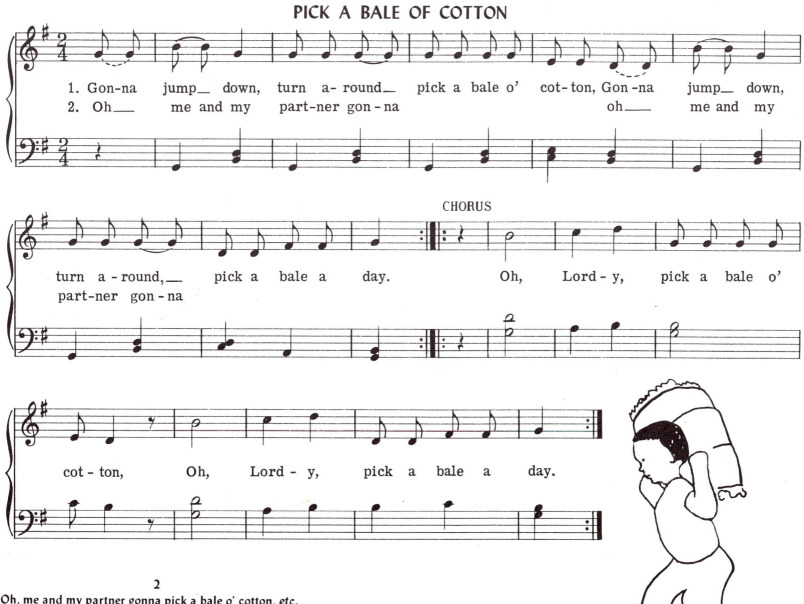

1. Gon-na jump_ down, turn a-round_ pick a bale o' cot-ton, Gon-na jump_ down,
2. Oh_ me and my part-ner gon-na oh_ me and my

CHORUS

turn a-round,_ pick a bale a day. Oh, Lord-y, pick a bale o'
part-ner gon-na

cot-ton, Oh, Lord-y, pick a bale a day.

2
Oh, me and my partner gonna pick a bale o' cotton, *etc.*

3
Oh, me and my neighbor gonna pick a bale o' cotton, *etc.*

4
I'm a-goin' down to Georgia for to pick a bale o' cotton, *etc.*

5
When I get to Heaven gonna pick a bale o' cotton, *etc.*

6
Oh, pick a bale o' pick a bale o' pick a bale o' cotton, *etc.*

JENNIE JENKINS

Oh, will you wear white, oh my dear, oh my dear, oh will you wear white Jen-nie Jen-kins? No, I'll not wear white, for the col-or's too bright, Gon-na buy me a fill-dy foll-dy, seek-a-dou-ble, use-a cause-a, Roll, the find me! Roll, Jen-nie Jen-kins, roll!

2

Oh, will you wear green, *etc.*

No, I'll not wear green, it's a shame to be seen, *etc.*

3

Oh, will you wear black, *etc.*

No, I'll not wear black, it's the color of my back, *etc.*

4

Oh, will you wear red, *etc.*

No, I'll not wear red, it's the color of my head, *etc.*

5

Oh, will you wear blue, *etc.*

No, I'll not wear blue, 'cause the color's too true, *etc.*

(more)

JENNIE JENKINS

6
Oh, will you wear purple, *etc.*
No, I'll not wear purple, it's the color of a turtle, *etc.*

7
Oh, will you wear yellow, *etc.*
No, I'll not wear yellow, for the color's too mellow, *etc.*

8
Well, what will you wear, *etc.*
It's nothing I'll wear, I'm a-gonna go bare, *etc.*

ACTION (all ages)

This fine foolish song can be dramatized in many ways. Very young children like to choose the order of the stanzas, based on the colors they themselves are wearing. Or, you may use the above order of the stanzas and tell the children to stand up as the colors they are wearing are mentioned. If the children are sitting on the floor as they sing, they can lie down and roll during last part of the refrain.

Older children dramatize the song in their manner of singing it. Have the boys ask the questions, singing lines one and two. The girls answer, singing lines three, four and five. Everyone together sings the sixth line as a chorus.

Children at any age enjoy making up new verses for Jennie Jenkins. We have heard clever ones: "Will you wear plaid?— The color's too mad!" And silly ones, like: "Will you wear maroon?—It's the color of a spoon!" And, inevitably: "Will you wear orange? It's the color of an orange!" But we have never seen a group which, when invited to do so, failed to enter the game of inventing new stanzas.

PAPER OF PINS
Music on next page

ACTION I (all ages)

Paper of Pins is ideal for acting out. Have two children play the roles while the group sings, or select a different pair to act out each stanza, or let all who wish pair off and act out the story in separate couples with no attempt to unify the action. This latter method not only gives everyone a chance to act, but provides an unselfconscious atmosphere for the shy child, as he sees that the others are busy acting and not watching his performance.

For a formal presentation for ages 10-11-12 this makes a delightful playlet, with humorous props and old-fashioned costumes that children can concoct for themselves. All the extra boys are friends of the suitor, and all the extra girls the attendants of the heroine. After the hero has sung and acted the first four measures of his stanzas, the heroine's attendants repeat the music, changing the words into an explanation: "He'll give to you a paper of pins, for that's the way his love begins." After he has sung and acted the second four measures, the girls' chorus echoes: "If you will marry him, him, him, if you will marry him." In the same way, when the heroine has sung her first four measures, the hero's friends repeat the music: "She'll not accept your paper of pins," and after the second half of the stanza, "And she'll not marry you, you, you, and she'll not marry you."

For Stanza 11, have the boys and girls of the chorus couple off and follow the hero and heroine off the stage in a grand march.

ACTION II (ages 4-5-6 and 7-8-9)

For an extremely simple singing game, put boys and girls in two lines, facing each other. For Stanzas 1, 3, 5, and 7 the boys move forward to girls, bow, return to place; repeat. For Stanzas 2, 4, 6, and 8 the girls do the same.

Stanza 9: Boys turn to left, following boy at the left end of their line. They march around the girls' line and back to place.

Stanza 10: Girls sit down on the floor and sing.

Stanza 11: Boys and girls opposite each other take hands

PAPER OF PINS

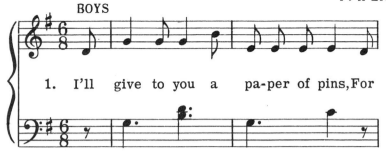

1. I'll give to you a pa-per of pins, For

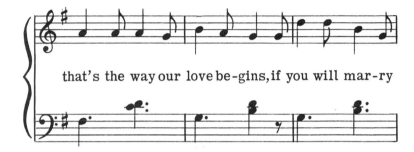

that's the way our love be-gins, if you will mar-ry

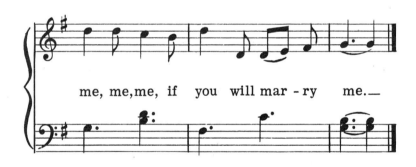

me, me, me, if you will mar-ry me.—

2 GIRLS:
I'll not accept your paper of pins
If that's the way your love begins,
And I'll not marry you, you, you,
    And I'll not marry you.

3 BOYS:
I'll give to you a house and land
And two spotted cows and one hired hand,
If you will marry me, me, me,
    If you will marry me.

4 GIRLS:
I'll not accept your house and land
Or two spotted cows or one hired hand,
And I'll not marry you, you, you,
    And I'll not marry you.

5 BOYS:
I'll give to you a gown of red
Stitched all around with golden thread,
If you will marry me, me, me,
    If you will marry me.

6 GIRLS:
I'll not accept your gown of red
Stitched all around with golden thread,
And I'll not marry you, you, you,
    And I'll not marry you.

7 BOYS:
I'll give to you the key to my chest
That you may have gold at your behest, *etc.*
If you will marry me, me, me,
    If you will marry me.

8 GIRLS:
I do accept the key to your chest
That I may have gold at my behest,
And I will marry you, you, you,
    And I will marry you.

9 BOYS:
Oh, I love coffee and you love tea,
You love my money but you don't love me,
So I'll not marry you, you, you,
    And I'll not marry you.

10 GIRLS:
Then I will be a wrinkled old maid,
I'll take my stool and sit in the shade,
If you'll not marry me, me, me,
    If you'll not marry me.

11 ALL:
I'll give to you the key to my heart
That we may be married and never part,
And I will marry you, you, you,
    And I will marry you.

and march in a big circle back to place—or march to their seats.

ACTION III (ages 7-8-9 and 10-11-12)

Any number of couples form two lines, about 4 feet apart. Every second couple the partners exchange places, so that each line now has boys and girls alternately, partners facing each other.

Stanzas 1, 3, 5, and 7: First four measures, boys walk three steps forward toward girls, bow, and walk three steps backward to place. Pantomime the nature of the gift, while doing so. Second four measures, boys move three steps toward their partners, joining right hands with them. The girls pivot to the right, turning under the arch made of their own and their partners' right arms. As girls complete the pivot, boys release their hands and step backward to their places.

Stanzas 2, 4, and 6: First four measures, girls move forward to partners and back to place, pantomiming the words. Fifth through eighth measures, partners do-si-do. (They walk past each other, brushing right shoulders, take one step to the right, and walk backward to their places brushing left shoulders as they pass.)

Stanza 8: First four measures, girls move forward and back, with pantomime, as above. Measures 5 through 8, partners walk toward each other, join right hands, go around each other once and back to place.

Stanza 9: First four measures, boys move toward partners and back. Second four measures, boys about face and walk four steps *away* from the set and four steps back to place.

Stanza 10: All girls take two steps forward and sit down on the floor, or pantomime sitting on a low stool. This places all the girls in one line down the center of the set, with a line of boys on either side. Girls remain seated through the end of the stanza. Boys face right and walk in an oval around the line of girls, counterclockwise. After four measures they about face and walk clockwise back to their places.

Stanza 11: Boys and girls sing. Boys take partners by both hands and pull them to their feet. All raise arms, so the set forms one continuous arch. The foot couple (the couple farthest from the piano, or simply the couple at the end designated to be the foot) walks under the arch, becoming part of the arch when it reaches the other end. The foot couple is immediately followed by the next and the next. It may be necessary to sing Stanza 11 two or three times so that every couple will have a turn at going through the arch.

KNICK KNACK

1. This old man,— he played one,— He played knick knack on my thumb—
Knees,clap, right, clap; knees, clap, ONE, clap; knees,clap, right,clap; knees,clap, THUMB, clap;

1. knick knack pad-dy whack, give your dog a bone, This old man came rol - ling home.
knees, cross, knees,—cross, knees,— cross, knees; Elbow swing._____

2
This old man, he played two,
He played knick knack on my shoe.
Knick knack, paddy whack, give your dog a bone,
This old man came rolling home.

3
This old man, he played three,
He played knick knack on my knee, *etc.*

4
This old man, he played four,
He played knick knack on the floor, *etc.*

5
This old man, he played five,
He played knick knack on a bee hive, *etc.*

6
This old man, he played six,
He played knick knack on some sticks, *etc.*

7
This old man, he played seven,
He played knick knack on his way to heaven, *etc.*

8
This old man, he played eight,
He played knick knack on my gate, *etc.*

9
This old man, he played nine,
He played knick knack on the line, *etc.*

10
This old man, he played ten,
He played knick knack in a pig pen, *etc.*

KNICK KNACK

ACTION I (ages 4-5-6 and 7-8-9)

This is a favorite with very young children. On the first line of each stanza they hold up fingers to indicate the number. On the second they pantomime the place, touching the floor, pointing up for heaven, etc. On the third line, they pat out the rhythm of *knick knack paddy whack* on their knees, and pantomime the throwing of a bone at the end of the line. The action for the fourth line depends on the amount of space available. If the children are sitting on the floor and there is plenty of room, let them actually roll about. If they are on chairs, or if the space is restricted, each child holds his fists before him and rotates them around each other.

ACTION II (ages 7-8-9 and 10-11-12)

In Boston we saw a large group of girls with individual jump ropes singing Knick Knack. One girl started, jumping in time to the first stanza. The last line was changed to, "Margaret may come rolling home." As the second stanza began, the first girl stopped and Margaret started to jump without missing a beat. At the end of her stanza Margaret sang, "Sally may come rolling home." Not one person, but the whole group, was considered the winner when they sang through ten with nobody's missing a step. At the end of the last stanza, since no one else could be invited in, they sang the traditional final line.

ACTION III (ages 7-8-9 and 10-11-12)

This is a game for two children, although many pairs can be arranged in a circle to make a large group game. Two children stand facing each other. They hit their hands against their own knees, then clap, then hit right hands, then clap, etc., through the first two lines. This familiar pattern may be varied in two places. Instead of the first left hand pat, they hold up fingers to indicate the number; and instead of the second left hand pat, they make some gesture to indicate the place.

During the third line each child hits his own knees, first hitting left knee with left hand and right with right, then

crossing hands to hit opposite knees, and so on. For the fourth line, each pair joins right elbows and swings.

The action for this game is written out under the music, but it is not suggested that these words be substituted for the traditional ones except, perhaps, in a learning session.

ROSELIL

Translation from Danish EOB

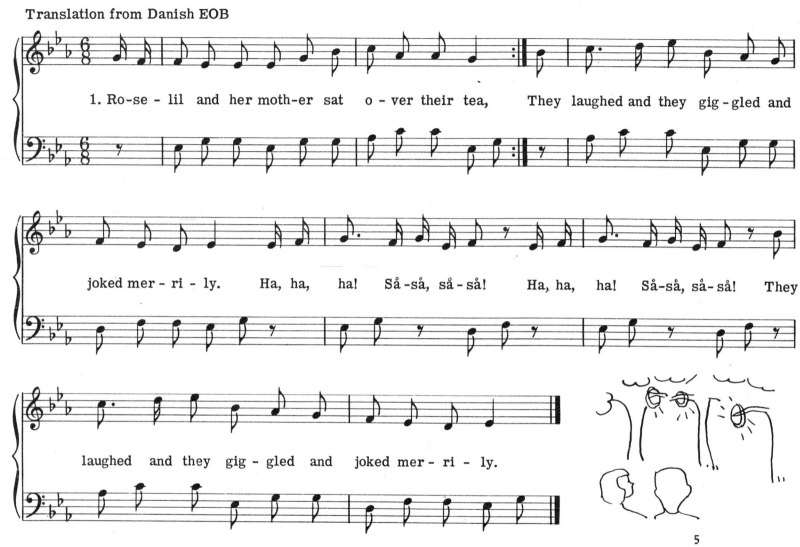

1. Ro-se - lil and her moth-er sat o - ver their tea, They laughed and they gig-gled and joked mer - ri - ly. Ha, ha, ha! Så-så, så-så! Ha, ha, ha! Så-så, så-så! They laughed and they gig - gled and joked mer - ri - ly.

2
"Not until our trees all have a blossom of gold,
Not until our trees all have a blossom of gold."
"Will I any man as my bridegroom behold!"
"Ha, ha, ha!" "Så-så, så-så!"
"Ha, ha, ha!" "Så-så, så-så!"
"Will I any man as my bridegroom behold!"

3
Herr Peder was eavesdropping most eagerly,
"For he who laughs last laughs best," said he.

4
Then he took her to the garden and what did they see?
He had hung a gold ring on every tree!

5
Roselil blushed as red as a blushing red rose,
She stared at the grass that lay green
'round her toes.

6
Herr Peder then kissed his love most eagerly,
"For he who laughs last laughs best," said he.

ROSELIL

ACTION (ages 10-11-12)

This is a singing game from Denmark, still danced in many a Danish-American community. Roselil is pronounced rosaleel. Pronounce sa-sa as *so-so*. Herr Peder is pronounced as follows: Herr (Mr.) is like the first syllable of the name *Harry;* the first syllable of Peder (Peter) rhymes with the word *there.* Everyone sings all the lines except for *Ha, ha, ha,* which is sung by the boys in a bragging manner, and *så-så, så-så,* which is sung by the girls. Teach the song well before attempting the game, or have several people sing while the others dance, trading off until all know the melody and words as well as the steps.

Form a circle, boys having their partners on the right. All hold hands throughout the game.

First line: Step left on left foot. Step left on right foot, crossing it behind the left. Step left on left. Hop on left, swinging right foot across in front. (One measure.) Then reverse the action: Step right on right foot. Step right on left foot, crossing it in front of the right. Step right on right. Hop in place on right, swinging the left foot across in front.

Second and third lines repeat the above actions, to the left and to the right on each line.

Fourth and fifth lines: All stand still, hands joined. Men turn toward partners and bow, singing *Ha, ha, ha.* Girls turn toward corners and bow, sing *så-så, så-så.* Repeat.

Sixth line: All take a short step to the left, left foot, then right (2 beats). Raise arms forward, rising on toes (2 beats), and down again (2 beats). Repeat on second measure.

POP GOES THE WEASEL

Music on next page

ACTION I (ages 4-5-6)

Preschool children play a combination singing game and dramatic improvisation to Pop Goes the Weasel. During the first stanza and the choruses, the children skip to the left in a circle, except for the weasel and his various victims. At the beginning of Stanza 2, the weasel touches one child who turns and starts to skip around outside the circle which is now standing still. The weasel follows through the hole and skips after him. At the word *pop,* he smacks the monkey on the bottom, and the monkey runs to his place. At the beginning of Stanza 3, the weasel chooses a possum. The possum pantomimes pulling up the covers and so forth, until the word *pop,* when the weasel tickles him and he runs to his place. For Stanza 4, the weasel picks a groundhog who crawls around looking for his hole. At the word *pop,* the weasel rushes toward him with some frightening gesture and he runs back to his place.

ACTION II (all ages)

Form two lines. They need not necessarily be boys and girls facing, but we will describe it in that way for convenience. The head of the set is at the boys' left, the girls' right. The figure is the same whether for verse or chorus. The head girl forms a circle of three with the second couple (the second boy takes his partner's left hand in his right and they hold out their free hands to the head girl). They circle around to the left until the word *pop,* at which time couple II makes an arch of the boy's right and the girl's left arms, and with their other hands they pop the head girl through the arch, down the set. It is essential that each person be popped *down* the set, not up the set or off to a side.

When the chorus begins, the head girl will circle with couple III and the head boy circles with couple II. When they have passed along to the next position, couple II, which is now the head couple, must clap out one stanza (or chorus) before the new head girl becomes active.

As a girl reaches the foot of the set she joins the girls' line, and when her partner arrives at the foot he joins the boys' line,

POP GOES THE WEASEL

1. A pen-ny for a spool of thread, A pen-ny for a nee-dle, That's where the

mon-ey goes, Pop goes the weas-el! A pen-ny for a spool of thread, A

CHORUS

pen-ny for a nee-dle, That's where the mon-ey goes, Pop goes the weas-el!

2
All around the cobbler's bench,
The monkey chased the weasel,
The monkey thought 'twas all in fun—
Pop goes the weasel!

3
The possum pulled the covers up,
Because he had the measles,
The quilt began to wiggle and bump—
Pop goes the weasel!

4
"It's time for bed," the groundhog says,
"I'll take it nice and easy."
But when he crawls into his hole—
Pop goes the weasel!

POP GOES THE WEASEL

so that they become the foot couple ready to pop the next player who comes along.

ACTION III (ages 10-11-12)

This is a play party for sets of four couples and is not essentially different from a square dance except that the players sing their own music. The following stanzas may be used while learning, but when the routine has been mastered, they should be discarded in favor of the traditional words:

These four stanzas are followed by a chorus, during which all players allemande left (that is, join left hands with corners and walk around them back to place) and a grand right and left (explained in Introduction). At the end of the chorus start immediately with Stanza 1, singing, "The *next* lady out to the right," for it is now the turn of couple II to be the head couple. Repeat for couple III and then for couple IV, always using four stanzas followed by one chorus for each round.

1

The first lady out to the right,
Now don't you dare to blunder,
Three hands around and around,
Pop the lady under.

First girl circles with couple two.

2

Lady go on, the gentleman follow,
Don't you dare to blunder,
Three hands around and around,
Pop them both right under.

First girl circles with couple three, while first boy circles with couple two.

3

On to the last, the gentleman follow,
Don't you dare to blunder,
Three hands around and around,
Pop them both right under.

First girl circles with couple four and first boy with couple three. When couple four pops the girl they do not release her hands, but pull her back through the arch again. Her partner joins the circle between the two girls, and this time they are popped through as a couple.

4

Lady come back and the gent come up,
Now don't you dare to blunder,
Four hands around and around,
Pop them both right under.

PIG IN THE PARLOR

We've got a new pig in the par-lor, we've got a new pig in the par-lor, we've
Your right hand to your part-ner, the left hand to your neigh-bor, your

got a new pig in the par-lor, and he's a good one, too!
right hand to the next one, your left one to the last!

And he's a good one, too! And he's a good one, too! (Your...)

ACTION (ages 7-8-9 and 10-11-12)

This play party from Indiana can be played by any number of couples. Form a circle with girls on the boys' right, and one extra person in the middle. Traditionally, the extra person is a boy, but if necessary the pig can be a girl and the song must say, "*She's* a good one, too!"

All the couples promenade during the first 12 measures, and do a grand right and left (as the words clearly indicate) during the final 8 measures. During the grand right and left, the pig slips into line hoping that when the song begins again he will have a partner. This will leave a new boy to be the pig in the parlor. If the same person ends up without a partner, the verse is changed to say: "The same old pig in the parlor."

The pig, trying to get a partner, and all the other boys as well, must keep time precisely and maintain the design of the grand right and left. This will not only prevent scuffling (which is taboo in a play party), but it will also preserve the dance character of the game.

A TISKET A TASKET

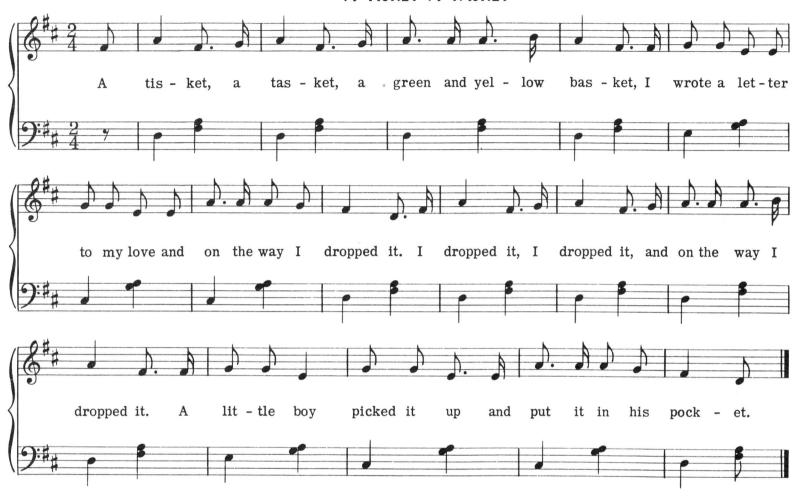

A tis - ket, a tas - ket, a green and yel - low bas - ket, I wrote a let - ter to my love and on the way I dropped it. I dropped it, I dropped it, and on the way I dropped it. A lit - tle boy picked it up and put it in his pock - et.

ACTION I (ages 4-5-6 and 7-8-9)

All but one form a circle, holding hands and singing the song. The one who is It has a handkerchief. He skips around the outside of the circle and drops the handkerchief behind any child he chooses. He then races around the circle in the same direction, while the child behind whom it was dropped runs in the opposite direction. Whichever gets back to the handkerchief first takes the empty place in the circle. The other picks up the handkerchief and starts over, waiting for the beginning words of the song.

Ordinarily, the handkerchief should be dropped some time between the eighth and twelfth measures, as the words indicate, and if it has been dropped behind a girl the last line is sung, "A little *girl* picked it up and put it in *her* pocket."

ACTION II (ages 10-11-12)

Like many games popular among the very young, this one will occasionally suit the fancy of much older children. Some years ago, with a little syncopation added, the entire song became a popular hit on the adult level.

PAWPAW PATCH

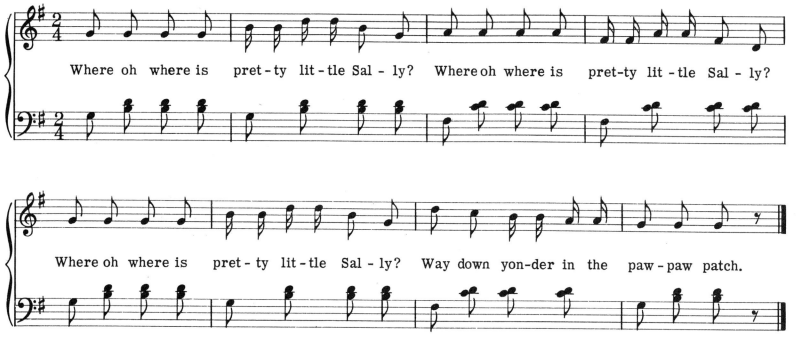

Where oh where is pret-ty lit-tle Sal-ly? Where oh where is pret-ty lit-tle Sal-ly?

Where oh where is pret-ty lit-tle Sal-ly? Way down yon-der in the paw-paw patch.

2
Come on, boys, let's go find her,
Come on, boys, let's go find her,
Come on, boys, let's go find her,
Way down yonder in the pawpaw patch.

3
Picking up pawpaws, put 'em in your pocket, *etc.*

4
Hold her tight so you won't lose her, *etc.*

PAWPAW PATCH

ACTION I (ages 4-5-6)

For very little children, Pawpaw Patch is a hide-and-seek game set to music. During the first stanza, all hold hands in front of their eyes, while Sally—or whoever else is named—skips to a hiding place. During Stanza 2, all the others skip about, trying to find her. Sing this stanza through as many times as needed until Sally is found. Children pantomime the third stanza, standing wherever they may be. For Stanza 4, all make a circle around Sally, joining hands, and skip back to the starting place.

This game is suitable for indoors or for a clearly limited outdoor area, and the tempo should be maintained at all times. Clever hiding places are not required, since the game is not competitive. Four- and five-year-olds are generally satisfied to play the ostrich, stooping in a corner with face turned away from the other players.

ACTION II (ages 7-8-9 and 10-11-12)

The most common of many play party arrangements of Pawpaw Patch requires a line of boys and a line of girls, about four feet apart, partners facing each other. The head of the set is at the left-hand end of the boys' line and the right-hand end of the girls' line.

Stanza 1: The head girl skips outside the set, down the girls' line, around the foot of the set, and back outside the boys' line, returning to her own place. If the lines of children are long, sing the stanza twice through to give her time.

Stanza 2: The head girl again skips outside the set, down the girls' line, but this time she is followed by the entire line of girls. At the same time, the head boy skips outside the set, down the boys' line, followed by all the boys. When the head couple meets at the foot of the set they make an arch, and the others join hands by couple as they pass through the arch and up toward the head of the set. Here, too, if there are many players you will have to sing the stanza twice. As this action ends, the second couple has become head couple and all the others have moved up one place, leaving the former head couple in foot position.

Stanza 3: Partners face each other, and all pantomime picking up pawpaws and putting them in pockets.

Stanza 4: Partners swing.

Some groups leave out the fourth stanza entirely. Some reverse the order of Stanzas 2 and 3. An alternate action for Stanza 4 is a promenade lead by the new head couple. They set out toward the boy's left and walk in a large circle back to place.

In all cases, the game ends when the first head couple has progressed all the way down the set and has regained the head of the set.

SKIP TO MY LOU

ACTION I (ages 4-5-6)

For very young children, form a circle with one child in the middle. As the game starts, he picks a partner and the two skip around while the circle sings and claps. In Stanza 1 the original child skips back into the circle and the new one skips around alone. For Stanza 2 she picks a partner, and they skip to the remainder of this stanza and to the chorus. Or you may substitute from 3 through 8 as alternatives for the chorus, in any order. Then immediately back to Stanzas 1 and 2, bringing a new child into the middle.

When singing Stanzas 3 through 8, children may do pantomime while skipping, or pantomime in tempo instead of skipping. Some groups have the partners skip, during these stanzas, while the members of the circle play act the words in their places.

ACTION II (ages 7-8-9)

Form two circles, all the children facing counterclockwise, in pairs. Skip this way for the chorus. For Stanza 1 those in the inside circle about-face (the boys, if you have boy-girl couples) and skip clockwise, while the outer circle continues to skip to the right. In Stanza 2 all stop, those in the inner circle turning about-face and taking as partners the adjacent member of the outer circle. The skipping resumes in pairs, counterclockwise, and continues during the singing of the chorus or any stanza from 3 through 8.

ACTION III (ages 7-8-9 and 10-11-12)

Form a circle of couples in promenade position. Skip counterclockwise for the chorus. Stop, all give right hands to partners, and grand right and left through Stanzas 1 and 2.

All will have new partners at this point (unless there are four or eight couples in the game). Sing any stanza, 3 through 8, while new partners swing with right elbows for the first two lines, then with left elbows for the second two lines. With the same new partner, skip in promenade position as the chorus is sung and the game begins again.

SKIP TO MY LOU

(CHORUS)

Skip,—— skip,—— skip to my lou, Skip,—— skip—— skip to my lou,

Skip,—— skip,—— skip to my lou, Skip to my lou, my dar - ling.

1
Lost my partner, what'll I do?
Lost my partner, what'll I do?
Lost my partner, what'll I do?
Skip to my lou, my darling.

2
I'll get another one, prettier than you.

3
Flies in the dairy, shoo, fly, shoo.

4
Cats in the buttermilk, two by two.

5
Mice in the bread tray, chew, mice, chew.

6
Doves in the hay mow, coo, bird, coo.

7
Pig in the parlor, what'll I do?

8
Cows in the mill pond, moo, cow, moo.

9
Roosters on the fence post, cockadoodle-doo.

TURN THE GLASSES OVER

I've been to Haar-lem, I've been to Do - ver, I have sailed this wide world o - ver.

O-ver, o-ver, three times o - ver, drink a glass of brand-y-wine and turn the glass-es o - ver.

Sail - ing east, sail - ing west, sail - ing o - ver the o - cean. Bet - ter watch

out when the boat be - gins to rock or you'll lose your part-ner in the o - cean!

TURN THE GLASSES OVER

ACTION I (ages 7-8-9 and 10-11-12)

Any number of couples form a circle with an extra person, usually but not necessarily a boy, standing in the middle. Boys stand toward the inside with their partners on their right. First eight measures, all promenade counterclockwise, holding hands (boy's right and girl's left).

Turning the glasses over is done as follows: Partners face each other, joining their free hands. They make an arch of the boy's left and girl's right arms and pass under, turning back to back as they go under. Both continue to turn in the same direction, raising an arch now of the boy's right and the girl's left arm and passing under this arch as they face each other. This action requires two measures and is done four times, measures 9 through 16.

At the words *sailing east,* the girls resume their counterclockwise promenade, but the boys turn heel and walk clockwise through the end of the song. During this section of the game, the odd boy from the middle joins the boys' promenade and hopes to end up with a partner, leaving a new boy to go to the middle as the game resumes at measure 1.

Note: It is possible to have two or even three boys (or girls) in the middle, if the number of players is great enough.

ACTION II (ages 10-11-12)

There are two interesting variations, either or both of which may be added to the foregoing.

One is to substitute a grand right and left for the two way promenade in the second half of the song.

The other change involves the first half of the song. Instead of simply holding hands during measures 1 through 8, take that promenade position in which left hands are joined in front and right hands are joined near the girl's right shoulder, the boy's right arm crossing behind her shoulders. This results in a different form of turning the glasses over in which a couple passes alternately under the arch created by their two left arms and then under their right arms.

CAROUSEL

ACTION I (ages 4-5-6)

This is a musical chairs game for little people. Take one chair fewer than the number of players and arrange them in a circle, facing out. During the first sixteen measures all players circle around outside the chairs, and on the word *late* all sit down. The child who is left without a place must go into the center of the circle, and the adult in charge removes one chair from the circle. During the four final measures, while the removal of the chair is going on, all those who are seated clap or stamp in time to their singing.

During the first sixteen measures of the next round, the child in the middle turns as the hub of the carousel. In later rounds, when two or more are in the middle, they join right hands and circle. In this way, those who fail to get seats are not eliminated, as in other games of musical chairs, but given a different role to play.

ACTION II (ages 7-8-9 and 10-11-12)

Form a double circle, boys on the inside. (This play party, like many others, does not necessarily require boy-girl couples. You may simply have the children form two concentric circles with equal numbers in each, regardless of sex.)

Measures 1 through 6: Boys (or inner circle) join left hands in the center and move counterclockwise. Each one grasps the wrist of the person in front of him to form a secure hub. Girls (or the outer circle) hold hands and move to the left, bending the left knee sharply at each left step. This gives them an up-and-down motion, as though they were the horses on the carousel.

Measures 7 through 12: Boys drop left hands and pivot in place clockwise. They now form a hub with right hands. The girls reverse their direction and bend the *right* knee on right steps to produce the rising and falling motion. At the end of this section, on the word *dime,* the girls drop hands and con-

tinue to move counterclockwise in single file, ready to hold out left hands to the boys in the inner circle.

Measures 13 through 16: Each boy (or member of the inner circle) holds out his left hand to the nearest girl (or member of the outer circle) who takes it in her left hand. The boy drops his right hand from the hub, pivots to the left, and puts his right arm around the girl's waist, clasping her right hand in his at the right side of her waist. Promenade. The turning figure does not take any time in itself. The girl, who was moving counterclockwise in the first place, continues in the same direction for the promenade without missing a step. The boy has reversed his direction without missing a step, and acquired a partner, too.

Measures 17 through 20: For children just learning play parties, continue the promenade during these four measures. For more experienced youngsters, this section calls for an allemand left (corners join left hands and walk around each other back to place), immediately followed by a grand right and left. As has been suggested elsewhere, do not teach this combination until your group can do a plain grand right and left with confidence and skill.

CAROUSEL

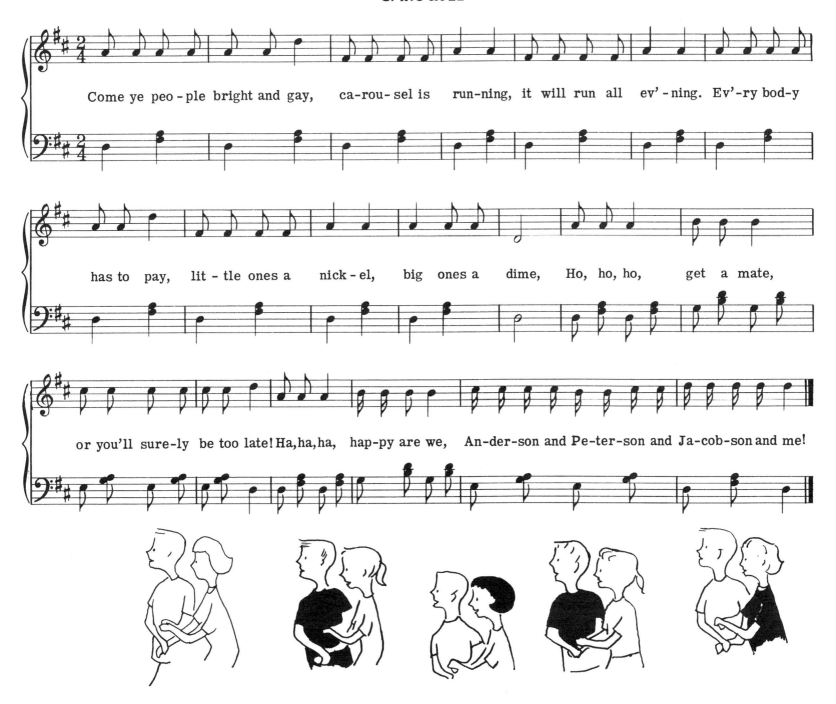

Come ye peo-ple bright and gay, ca-rou-sel is run-ning, it will run all ev'-ning. Ev'-ry bod-y

has to pay, lit-tle ones a nick-el, big ones a dime, Ho, ho, ho, get a mate,

or you'll sure-ly be too late! Ha, ha, ha, hap-py are we, An-der-son and Pe-ter-son and Ja-cob-son and me!

LITTLE BROWN JUG

ACTION I (ages 7-8-9 and 10-11-12)

Young children in Tennessee play Little Brown Jug using all the stanzas given here and more that they make up as they go along. Any number of couples form a circle, boys on the inside, all facing counterclockwise. For the first four measures of Stanza 1 skip in promenade formation; measure five, the girl pantomimes raising a glass and on the sixth measure, the boy does so. Right elbow swing for measures seven and eight.

Chorus: Couples stand facing each other, boys having their backs towards the center of the circle. Boys raise both arms over heads on measure one, slapping their thighs on the downbeat of measure two, and continuing in this rather slow, exaggerated pantomime of laughter throughout the eight measures.

The girls do the same, but they start by slapping their thighs on measure one and stretching arms up on measure two, etc. Thus, the girls are always bending and slapping their thighs while the boys are reaching up, and *vice versa*.

Stanza 2: First four measures, couples face each other and do strictly rhythmical shadow boxing; on measure five the girl raises an imaginary cup and on measure six the boy does the same. On measure seven, the girl puts her hands on her hips and at the word *her* stamps her right foot; the boy does the same on measure eight, stamping at the word *me*.

Stanza 3: First four measures, skip in promenade formation. During measures five and six, the boys pull forward while girls pull back—this is a pantomime, not a real tug-o'-war. For the last two measures couples face each other, the girl making scolding gestures with right fore finger, the boy impatiently tapping his foot.

Stanza 4: First four measures, skipping. Measures five and six demand pantomime of buying and selling. (Incidentally, *corn* is pronounced more like *cone* and refers to a liquid form of the grain.) For the last two measures, a right elbow swing.

ACTION II (ages 10-11-12)

Any number of couples in a circle, boys facing out, girls in. For instruction, have the group sing the words printed in italics under the music. Partners hold hands. First four measures, heel-and-toe on the boy's left foot and the girl's right foot, and slide to the boy's left. Next four measures repeat the action in the opposite direction. Only the first four measures of the chorus have the hand clapping. The final four measures are a right elbow swing at the end of which each boy steps one pace to his right and joins hands with a new partner. There is no pause between the end of the chorus and the next heel-and-toe.

LITTLE BROWN JUG

1. Me and my wife live all a-lone, In a lit-tle log hut we call our own,
Heel and toe Heel and toe Slide slide slide slide,

She loves whis-key, I love rum, And both to-geth-er we sure have fun!
Heel and toe Heel and toe Slide slide slide slide,

REFRAIN

First
Ha, ha, ha,— thee and me, Lit-tle brown jug how I love thee! I love thee!
time: Knees, clap, right, clap; knees, clap, left clap; Knees, clap, right, clap, left, clap, both!

2
Me and my wife we had a fight,
Whooped and hollered half the night—
She loves coffee and I love tea,
What does for her won't do for me!

3
Me and my wife and my wife's pap
Took a trip to Cumberland Gap.

Pappy wouldn't stop and muley wouldn't go
My wife she said, "I told you so!"

4
Me and my wife, we went down,
Took us a trip to Taz'well Town,
Sold our tobacco and bought us some corn
And both together we danced back home.

FROGGIE WENT A COURTIN'

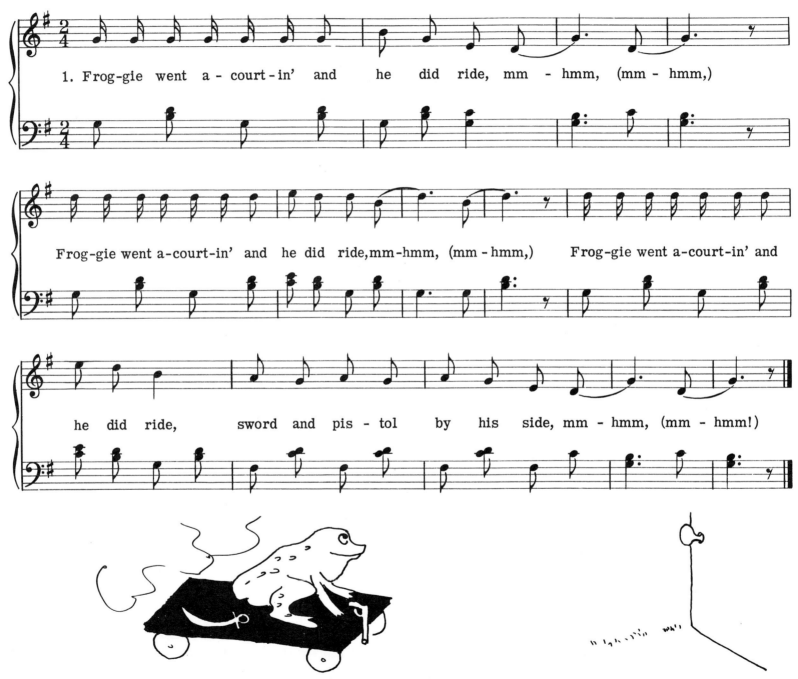

1. Frog-gie went a-court-in' and he did ride, mm - hmm, (mm - hmm,)

Frog-gie went a-court-in' and he did ride, mm-hmm, (mm - hmm,)   Frog-gie went a-court-in' and

he did ride,   sword and pis - tol   by   his   side, mm - hmm, (mm - hmm!)

FROGGIE WENT A COURTIN'

2
Rode up to Miss Mousey's door, ho-ho, (ho-ho,)
Rode up to Miss Mousey's door, ho-ho, (ho-ho,)
Rode up to Miss Mousey's door,
Where he'd often been before, ho-ho! (ho-ho!)

3
Said Miss Mousey are you within, ah-hah? (ah-hah?)
Yes, kind sir, I sit and spin, tee-hee! (tee-hee!)

4
Took Miss Mousey on his knee, mm-hmm, (mm-hmm,)
Said, Miss Mousey will you marry me? Please do! (Please do!)

5
Without my Uncle Rat's consent, oh no, (oh no,)
I would not marry the president, oh no! (oh no!)

6
Uncle Rat laughed till he shook his fat sides, ha-ha, (ha-ha,)
To think that his niece would be a bride, ha-ha! (ha-ha!)

7
Where shall the wedding supper be, mm-hmm, (mm-hmm,)
Down in the swamp in the holler 'simmon tree, mm-hmm!
    (mm-hmm!)

8
What shall the wedding supper be? yum-yum! (yum-yum!)
Fried mosquito and a black-eyed pea, yum-yum! (yum-yum!)

9
First to come in was a mealy moth, mm-hmm, (mm-hmm,)
And she laid out the table cloth, ah-hah! (ah-hah!)

10
Next to come in was a doodley bug, mm-hmm, (mm-hmm,)
And he was totin' that little brown jug, glub, glub! (glub, glub!)

11
Next to come in was a bumberly bee, b-zzz, (b-zzz,)
With a big bass fiddle on his knee, b-zzz! (b-zzz!)

12
Next to come in was a cumberly cow, moo-oo, (moo-oo,)
Tried to dance but she didn't know how, moo-oo! (moo-oo!)

13
Next to come in was a pussily cat, me-ow, (me-ow,)
He ate up the frog and the mouse and the rat, me-ow! (me-ow!)

14
Cornbread and clabber milk settin' on the shelf, mm-hmm,
    (mm-hmm,)
If you want any more you can sing it for yourself, that's all!
    (that's all)

ACTION (all ages)

The syllables at the end of the first, second, and fourth lines of each stanza are sung first by the song leader, then echoed by the group. The song leader may also invent gestures to go with each sound, in which case, the group will imitate the action as well as the sounds.

When the group is familiar with the song, try pointing to a different child at the start of each stanza who will sing syllables of his own choice at the ends of the lines, to be imitated by the entire group.

This is also a fine song to act out, with children playing the roles in pantomime while the inactive ones sing the verses. For this game, have the actors sing the nonsense syllables.

SEND MY BROWN JUG DOWN TO TOWN

Send my brown jug down to town, Send my brown jug down to town, Send my brown jug
Bring it back with a roll a-round, Bring it back with a roll a-round, Bring it back with a

down to town, Ev'-ry night when the sun goes down. Oh,___ no,___ what shall I
roll a-round, Ev'-ry night when the sun goes down.

do? Lost my true love, don't know where to find her. Well, she's gone, gone,

gone! Let her go, go, go! For she's gone on the rag-ing can-oe!___

SEND MY BROWN JUG DOWN TO TOWN

ACTION I (ages 4-5-6 and 7-8-9)

All form a circle, with one boy in the middle. All hold hands. First four measures, members of the circle move in toward the center, raising their joined hands high. Next two measures, back to place. On measures five through eight, repeat.

The boy in the middle picks a partner, and during the next eight measures the circle members sing and clap while the two in the middle do the following: For four measures they skip around each other holding right hands; then for four measures they skip in the opposite direction holding left hands.

At the words, *Oh, no,* the girl, followed by the boy, skips out of the circle under the arms of any two children, back into the circle between the next pair, and so on until the words *Well, she's gone.* At that point, or as soon thereafter as the girl is inside the circle and the boy outside, the ring turns clockwise, all the children quite close together so that the boy cannot get inside to find his partner. On the word *canoe,* the boy takes a place as part of the circle and the game begins again with the girl as the one in the middle. This time, and every other round, change the words to say, "Don't know where to find *him.* Well, *he's* gone, gone, gone! Let *him* go, go, go! For *he's* gone on the raging canoe."

ACTION II (ages 10-11-12)

Any number of couples in a circle, in promenade position. First eight measures, promenade. Next eight measures, all partners swing. Next eight measures, grand right and left. At the first word *gone,* each person should be ready to meet a new partner with right hands. All do an allemand right (that is, go all the way around this new partner with right hands joined). This takes two measures. All meet their new corners with left hands and do an allemand left (corners walk all around each other, holding left hands, and end up facing their partners). This takes two measures. Next two measures, partners do-si-do (pass each other brushing right shoulders, take a step to the right, and walk backwards passing each other by left shoulders). Final two measures, all sung on the last syllable of the word *canoe,* corners do-si-do.

All immediately take position with new partner for the promenade as the play party begins again without pause.

Note: If there are four couples in the game, the grand right and left will end with original partners reunited; if there are eight couples, original partners will be together every other round. If you can't avoid this situation, you can change the final sequence so that after the final do-si-do with corners, the corners set out together in the promenade, thus becoming new partners.

FARM BOY'S BONNY

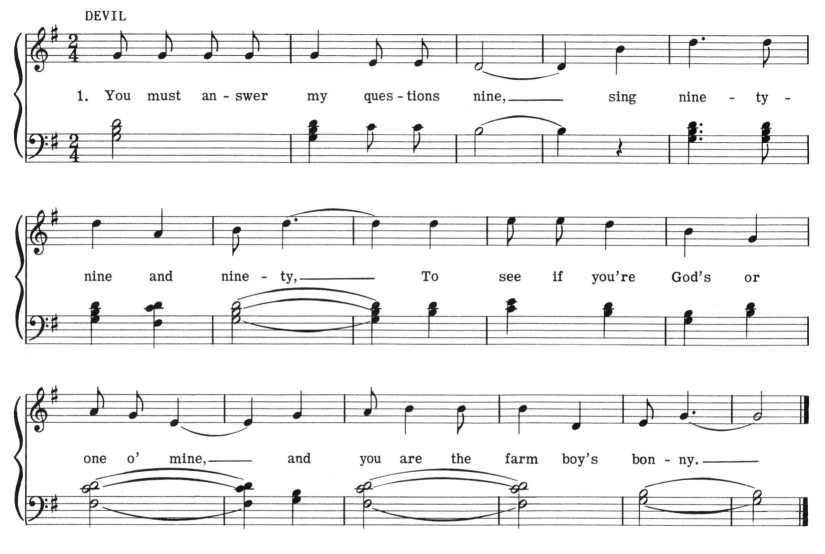

DEVIL

1. You must an-swer my ques-tions nine, _____ sing nine-ty-
nine and nine-ty, _____ To see if you're God's or
one o' mine, _____ and you are the farm boy's bon-ny. _____

2 DEVIL:
What is whiter than the milk? Sing ninety-nine and ninety!
And what is softer than the silk? And you are the farm boy's bonny!

3 GIRL:
Snow is whiter than the milk, sing ninety-nine and ninety!
And feathers are softer than the silk, and I am the farm boy's bonny!

4 DEVIL:
What is higher than a tree?
And what is deeper than the sea?

5 GIRL:
Heav'n is higher than a tree,
And Hell is deeper than the sea.

6 DEVIL:
What is stouter than an ox?
And what is slier than a fox?

7 GIRL:
Love is stronger than an ox,
And hate is slier than a fox.

FARM BOY'S BONNY

8 DEVIL:
What is louder than a horn?
And what is sharper than a thorn?

9 GIRL:
Thunder is louder than a horn,
And death is sharper than a thorn.

10 DEVIL:
What's more innocent than a lamb?

11 GIRL:
A babe's more innocent than a lamb.

12 DEVIL:
You have answered my questions nine,
And you are God's and none o' mine.

ACTION (ages 7-8-9 and 10-11-12)

The most immediate action demanded by this song is a division into parts, with the boys singing the devil's questions and the girls singing the answers. Later, try a soloist or a small group of boys for the devil, and a soloist or a small group of girls for the farm boy's bonny. Then the remainder of the children can take *Sing ninety-nine and ninety* as a chorus.

Singing the song this way will soon develop into further dramatics. Let the children work out pantomime for the various questions and answers which all will learn and perform simultaneously. Or pick different soloists for each stanza and let the soloists do the pantomime. Or work this out as a playlet, with actors for the two characters and the rest of the group to sing, boys and girls separately.

We have seen *The Farm Boy's Bonny* performed at a school assembly, for Hallowe'en, with costumes, sound effects, and plenty of red spot lights. In this case, they had a third character, the farm boy himself. Before the first stanza, there was a pantomime struggle between the devil and the girl. Every time the devil got too close, the girl fell to her knees and prayed. This made the devil retreat. But whenever the devil withdrew, the girl would start to go off with the farm boy and the devil returned. This was accompanied by thunderous music, flashes of lightning, and even a sulphurous smell suggesting some help from the science teacher. In this performance, there were no properties. The children in the chorus acted out milking and wearing silk, falling snow and sleeping on featherbeds. A real trumpet accompanied Stanza 8 and very real-sounding thunder came in Stanza 9. For the second half of Stanza 10 the chorus produced a tableau of the nativity. The devil disappeared and the red lights with him during the last line of Stanza 11, leaving the farm boy and his bonny in blue lights for the finale.

Although we listed this song for the two upper age levels, we have known younger children who loved it and who did beautiful free interpretations of the words while singing it.

MY GOOD OL' MAN

Where are ye go-in', my good ol' man? Where are ye go-in', my hon-ey, my lamb? Best ol' soul in the world! *(Spoken:)* Goin' fishin'!

2

When ye comin' back, my good ol' man?
When ye comin' back, my honey, my lamb?
Best ol' soul in the world!
    Spoken: Friday evenin'.

3

What ye want for supper, *etc.*
    Spoken: Eggs.

4

How many do ye want, *etc.*
    Spoken: Bushel.

5

Bushel will kill ye, *etc.*
    Spoken: Don't keer if hit do.

6

Where do ye want to be buried at, *etc.*
    Spoken: Chimbley corner.

7

Ashes will fall on ye, *etc.*
    Spoken: Hit don't matter.

8

Why do ye want to be buried there, *etc.*
    Spoken: So's I can haunt ye!

9

Haunt can't haunt a haunt, my good ol' man!
Haunt can't haunt a haunt, my honey, my lamb!
MEANEST OL' DEVIL IN THE WORLD!

MY GOOD OL' MAN

ACTION I (all ages)

Here is another song the mere singing of which is dramatic. Have the girls sing the three lines of each stanza, while the boys give the spoken response. Or choose one boy with a deep, gruff voice to be the old man, and let everyone else do the singing part. Or, have everybody sing with the understanding that during each stanza you will point to someone to speak the old man's words at the end. In the latter way, eight people can have a turn at being the old man in one rendition of the song. Stanza 9, naturally, has no response. The woman has the last word.

When we heard this done in Kentucky, the person playing the old man spoke in a gruff, bored monotone, never raising his voice or having any expression until Stanza 8. They pronounced the key word *ha'nt* (to rhyme with can't). The song is something of a riddle. Whether the old woman is saying that she is a ghost, right then and there, or whether she is implying that when he dies she'll die of sorrow, is anybody's guess. As we heard it sung, the old woman's song was calm, loving and tender, until Stanza 9.

ACTION II (all ages)

My Good Ol' Man is also dramatized in a singing game. Choose one boy to be the first old man, and have everyone (including the chosen boy) form a circle, each person having arms around the waists of those on either side. The action of the circle is simply to sway, left on the left foot in the first measure, right on the right foot in the next, and so forth, always returning the feet to the same place. No swaying during the spoken responses.

At the end of Stanza 1, the chosen boy walks into the middle, says his line, and sits down on the floor. During the singing of the next stanza, he nods at another boy, who joins him when that stanza ends and speaks the second response. This boy chooses the third, and so forth, until there are seven boys sitting in a small circle, facing out toward the big circle, during the singing of Stanza 8. No new boy is selected to come out at the end of this verse. Instead, all seven say the response at the end of Stanza 8 in unison, leaping to their feet on the words *haunt ye*.

During the singing of Stanza 9, the seven old men try to escape by diving between the legs of the children forming the circle.

FARMER IN THE DELL

1. The far-mer in the dell,— the far-mer in the dell,— Hi ho the derr-i-o, The far-mer in the dell.—

2
The farmer takes a wife, the farmer takes a wife,
Hi ho, the derrio, the farmer takes a wife.

3	**7**
The wife takes a child.	The cat takes a rat.
4	
The child takes a nurse.	**8**
5	The rat takes a cheese.
The nurse takes a dog.	
6	**9 (or 16)**
The dog takes a cat.	The cheese stands alone.

ACTION (ages 4-5-6 and 7-8-9)

All but one child form a circle and march to the left. The farmer chooses a wife, the wife a child, etc. For a short game, sing "The cheese stands alone" as Stanza 9. During this stanza, the children forming the circle stand still and clap, and all those in the middle run away and rejoin the circle, leaving the cheese to start the next game as the farmer.

For a longer game, the ninth stanza goes, "The farmer runs away," Stanza 10 goes, "The wife runs away," and so on, with "The cheese stands alone" coming out as Stanza 16.

Actually, whether the long or short version is used, there are two quite different approaches to this game, and most groups of children enjoy playing both. One way is to play it as a rhythm game, with little or no play-acting. The circle marches with accented rhythm from the first note until the clapping out of the cheese; those in the middle form a curving line, led by the farmer, and also march in time without a pause. The other approach is to eliminate the marching and substitute pantomime. For example, the farmer walks with big strides, hoeing or sowing seeds. The wife may play at churning, knitting or washing dishes. The child skips about. The nurse cuddles the child. The remaining parts are animals which the children will know how to perform.

ACTION II (ages 7-8-9 and 10-11-12)

Older children sometimes enjoy assembling props for the actors. Help them find—or improvise—a rake for the farmer, knitting bag for the wife, any toy for the child, doll carriage for the nurse, a leash for the dog, a bell or a ribbon for the cat, a long rope to be held as a tail for the rat and a sign saying CHEESE for the last actor. Have these props in a pile in the middle of the ring so the children can pick them up as they are selected for the roles.

For a very special occasion, children can put together costumes for a performance of *Farmer in the Dell*. This makes a fine party stunt which can be prepared, rehearsed and performed inside half an hour—if the adults provide old clothes, paper bags for masks, scissors, crayons and safety pins.

TURKEY IN THE STRAW (Virginia Reel)

(MUSIC ON NEXT TWO PAGES)

ACTION I (ages 6-7-8 and 9-12)

The Virginia Reel is one of the few complicated long-way dances (with two straight lines) which is commonly seen as a play party. The reason is that there are always a good number of people not involved in the action who can sing the music. The active couples can hardly find breath for both dancing and song. Some people use the dance words that are printed above; others use these words only while teaching the dance and sing any of the humorous stanzas thereafter, depending on the players to know the action by heart. Whichever you use, always sing three stanzas, then the chorus twice, and then a fourth stanza. This completes one round. You will need as many rounds as there are couples in the largest set.

Have five to eight couples in a set. If you have nine couples or more, have several sets. Boys on one side, girls on the other, partners facing each other. The end of the to the boys' left and the girls' right is the head of the set. The other end is the foot.

The head girl and the foot boy go toward each other, bow, and back to place. The head boy and foot girl repeat. Repeat, turning each other with right hands, with left hands, with both hands. Repeat with a do-si-do (head girl and foot boy walk past each other, brushing right shoulders, take a short step to the right, and walk backward to place brushing left shoulders as they pass.) Foot boy and head girl do the same. Then the head couple joins hands and slides down the aisle to the foot of the set and back. Hook right elbows ready to reel.

Reeling: Done to the singing of the chorus. Head couple turns by right elbows 1½ times around. The girl turns the next boy by left elbows while the boy turns the next girl by left elbows. One turn, and the head couple meets in the aisle, turns once with right elbows, then left elbows to the sides, right elbows together, left to the sides, until they have progressed to the foot of the set, turning each side person in turn by left and alternately turning each other by right. Reeling is most effective when the side person who is next in line steps forward

with left arm out to meet the reeler. This helps the reeler who is sometimes too excited, sometimes too dizzy, to know who is next!

In some play parties reeling ends when the head couple reaches the foot of the set. (For example, see *Down the River,* the next game.) In the Virginia Reel, when the head couple has reeled to the foot, they turn each other a last time, join hands, and walk or slide back to the head of the set for the march. The reeling is done to the singing two times of the chorus.

The march: The head boy turns to the left and walks down the boys line on the outside, followed by all the boys. At the same time, the girl turns to the right and leads the girls' line outside itself to the foot. The head couple joins hands to make an arch. The others pass under, each couple temporarily joining hands, and form lines. This puts the number two couple in the head position, each other couple moved up one place, and the former head couple is now foot couple.

ACTION II (ages 4-5-6)

The Virginia Reel can be done by very young children with the reeling omitted. Simply go from the end of Stanza 3, down the center and back, to Stanza 4, the march.

However, the humorous traditional stanzas are more fun for little children than the dance words. They will learn other stanzas at home and make up still more themselves, and the words will encourage actions of their own.

TURKEY IN THE STRAW (Virginia Reel)

SONG: 1. Oh as I was a com-in' on down the road, With a

DANCE: 1. Oh the head la-dy bal-ance and you come right back, And the
2. Oh the head la-dy leads with a left hand turn, And the
3. Now the head la-dy dou-bles with a do si do, And the
4. Oh, you march out - side on the out - side track, And you

SONG: tir-ed team and a heav-y load, Oh, I cracked my whip and the

DANCE: head gent fol-low on the same old track, Now the head la-dy right hand
head gent fol-low or you'll nev-er learn, And the head la-dy cross-es in a
head gent dou-bles just the same, you know, Now the head cou-ple down the set, with
make your feet go whick-et-y whack, Oh, the head cou-ple arch-es at the

SONG: lead-er sprung, And I said day day to the wag-on tongue!

DANCE: once a - round, And the head gent will do the same, or I'll be bound!
two - hand whirl, And the head gent will fol-low with that pret-ty lit-tle girl!
toe and heel, And you slide right back a-gain and start to reel!
bot-tom of the set, And the oth-ers dou-ble un-der and you'll get there yet!

2

Oh I came to the river and I couldn't get across   Well, he wouldn't go ahead and yet he wouldn't go back,
So I paid ten dollars for a big bay hoss,   But he went up and down just like a steeple jack.

Tur-key in the hay, (whistle) tur-key in the straw,

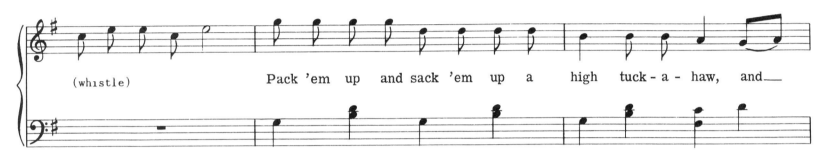

(whistle) Pack 'em up and sack 'em up a high tuck - a - haw, and___

whis-tle up a num-ber called The Tur-key in the Straw.

3
Oh, I jumped on the seat and I gave a little shout,
And the bed tumbled in and the wheels fell out,
And the harness fell apart and the hosses run away
And I doubt if I'll get home afore the break of day.

4
Oh, I went out to milk but I didn't know how,
And I milked the cat instead of the cow,
So I went to the pig sty to gather up some eggs
But I came back a-carrying a turkey leg.

5
Down in the ditch by the Portland road
I met Mr. Bullfrog, I met Miss Toad,
And every time Missy Toad would sing
Mr. Bullfrog cut a pigeon wing.

6
Oh, the crow is in the corn crib, setting on a chair,
Just a-counting all the corn and a-combing of his hair,
And the rabbit's in the pea patch picking up peas—
But I thought I heard that chicken sneeze.

DOWN THE RIVER

ACTION I (ages 4-5-6)

Place children in two lines about 6 feet apart. Spread the lines so as to provide at least an arm's length between neighbors. The head couple puts arms around each other's waists and gives free hands to the number II children on the side lines. The II's pull the head couple along down the set, handing them on to the number III couple at the end of the second measure. The children on the side lines do not move from their places, simply moving their arms as they help the active couple along. The head couple is a boat, their outside arms the oars. When the head couple reaches the foot of the set, they join the side lines, one on either side.

At the beginning of the chorus, the second couple starts down the river, and thereafter each time a verse or chorus begins, a new couple sets out. The action must be smooth and rhythmic, never rough. Even if you sing the song quite fast, the boats will not move too quickly.

For more than ten or twelve couples, bend the lines around to form a horseshoe, and in a big space with a great many couples we have seen the "river" in a big S curve—more like the Tennessee than the Ohio, but lots of fun.

ACTION II (ages 7-8-9 and 10-11-12)

Any number of couples in two lines, boys on one side, girls on the other, partners facing. Head of the set is toward the boys' left, the girls' right. Head couple reels, turning each other 1½ times by right elbows, then the sides (couple II) with left elbows, each other with right, couple III with left, each other with right, and so on. This figure is described more fully in the previous game, under the Virginia Reel. As the head couple reaches the foot of the set, it separates and joins the sides, becoming the foot couple.

In the meantime, as the chorus begins, couple II starts to reel down the set. When the verse begins again, couple III sets out, and at the next chorus, couple IV.

If the players keep strict time, all the active couples will be turning each other in the aisle at the same time, and they all will separate to turn the side players at the same time. For example, when the first chorus begins, couple I will turn each other, prior to turning couple IV; at the same time, couple II will turn each other, prior to turning couple III. By the time half the couples have set out down the river, all players will be busy, because one reeling couple will always be abreast of each side couple.

With a young or relatively inexperienced group of children, start the next couple only at the beginning of each verse. When they have mastered the figure thoroughly, then teach them to start a boat at the beginning of every chorus as well.

DOWN THE RIVER

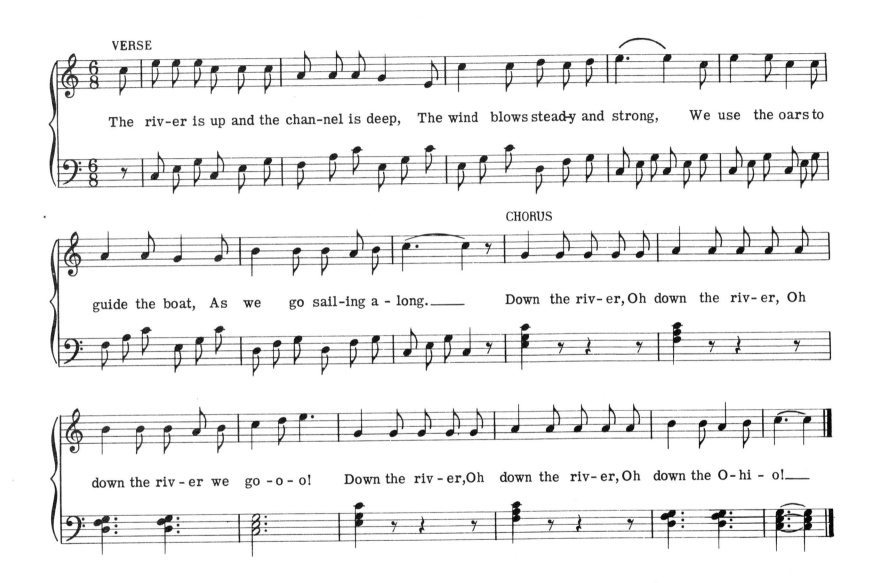

VERSE

The riv-er is up and the chan-nel is deep, The wind blows stead-y and strong, We use the oars to guide the boat, As we go sail-ing a - long.____

CHORUS

Down the riv-er, Oh down the riv-er, Oh down the riv-er we go-o-o! Down the riv-er, Oh down the riv-er, Oh down the O-hi - o!____

WAY UP IN THE HOLLER

1. Way up in the hol - ler, By the side of the Clinch, You__ lead and I'll
2. When we get to - geth - er, By the side of the Clinch, We'll stroll down to -

fol - ler, By the side of the Clinch.
geth - er, By the side of the Clinch.

3. Oh, you swing her and you leave her, By the

side of the Clinch, Oh, you swing her and you leave her By the side of the Clinch.

WAY UP IN THE HOLLER

ACTION I (ages 4-5-6 and 7-8-9)

Form two lines about four feet apart, boys facing girls. The boy at the left end and the girl at the right end are the head couple.

Stanza 1: Head boy turns left and strolls outside the boys' line, while the head girl turns right and strolls outside the girls' line. Repeat the stanza if necessary to bring them unhurriedly to the foot of the set.

Stanza 2: They link arms and stroll up the aisle back to their place at the head. Repeat the stanza, as needed.

Stanza 3: The music is twice as fast. The head couple does an elbow swing for the first line of music, then separates and the boy and girl skip quickly down the outside of the set and take positions as the foot couple.

Some people have *all* the couples do a right elbow swing during the first line of this stanza. Repeat the music if necessary, so that the couple has taken its place at the foot before starting the game again with the next head couple.

ACTION II (ages 7-8-9 and 10-11-12)

The figure for Stanzas 1 and 2 is identical with the game described above for younger children. The figure for Stanza 3 is a reel. Repeat the stanza until the head couple has reeled to the foot. There the boy joins the boys' line and the girl joins the girls' so that they now form the foot couple. To reel, the head couple links right elbows and turns 1½ times. The girl turns the first side boy with left elbow while the boy turns the first side girl with left elbow. Meet in the center and turn each other by right, separate and turn the next pair by left, and so on, down to the foot of the set.

In playing *Way Up in the Holler,* or even in singing it without activity, note the contrast between the slow, waltzy character of the first two stanzas and the quick jig-time of Stanza 3.

(Clinch Mountain and Clinch River run from southwestern Virginia into Tennessee.)

OLD JOE CLARKE

1. I went down to old Joe's house, He met me at the door, Shoes and stock-ings in his hand, And his feet all o-ver the floor!

CHORUS

Fare you well, Old Joe Clarke, Fare you well, I say! Fare you well, Old Joe Clarke, I ain't got long to stay!

2
I went down to Old Joe's house,
Never been there before,
He slept on the corn shuck bed
And I slept on the floor.

3
I went down to old Joe's house,
He told me come and eat,
I drank all the clabber milk
And he ate all the meat.

4
I played cards with Old Joe Clarke,
I'll never be the same,
All he got when he dealt them out
Was high, low, jack and game.

5
When I was a little bitty gal,
I used to play with toys.
Now I am a great big gal
And I'd rather play with boys.

OLD JOE CLARKE

6

If you see that gal of mine,
Tell her to come right home,
Tell her old Joe Clarke done gone
And I'm waiting here alone.

7

If I had a pretty little gal,
I'd set her on the shelf,
And every time she smiled at me
I'd climb up there myself.

CHORUS

Fare you well, old Joe Clarke,
Fare you well, I say!
Fare you well, old Joe Clarke,
I ain't got long to stay.

ACTION I (ages 4-5-6)

This song has an irresistible rollick that makes little children move. Whether they use it to act out the words or simply for rhythmic play, they're sure to like it. If they find making up new stanzas difficult, encourage them to invent new chorus lines instead. There are many traditional ones, such as "Rock-a-rock, old Joe Clarke, Rock-a-rock, you're gone, Rock-a-rock, old Joe Clarke, and good bye Betsy Brown."

ACTION II (ages 7-8-9 and 10-11-12)

Old Joe Clarke is one of our most commonly used square dance tunes, but we know one quick-change play party version. Adults would never have the breath to play and sing this one simultaneously, but we have seen children do it till they were ready to drop. Use these special words, while teaching it, but then go back to the humorous stanzas or help your group make up their own:

VERSE: Left hand round your corner gal,
               Right hand round your own,
               Do-si-do that corner gal,
               And do-si-do your own.

CHORUS: Promenade that corner gal,
                 Fare you well, I say!
                 Promenade, old Joe Clark,
                 I ain't got long to stay.

Since you always promenade your corner, who becomes your partner for the ensuing stanza, partners change every sixteen measures. Form a circle of any number of couples in promenade position, boys toward the center of the circle with their partners on their right. Start with a promenade to the tune of the chorus, using any words you please, and then go into the special words printed above.

Besides being fun in itself, this is one of the play parties where partners change so quickly that there is no need to have the children pick partners. Simply form a line of boys and a line of girls at random and start the game. This sort of play party is also useful as a means of setting up couples for some other play party in which partners really dance together. If your group is at an age where picking partners is difficult, simply play Old Joe Clarke as long as you wish, and when you stop tell all players that they are to stay with present partners for the next play party.

OATS, PEAS, BEANS AND BARLEY GROW

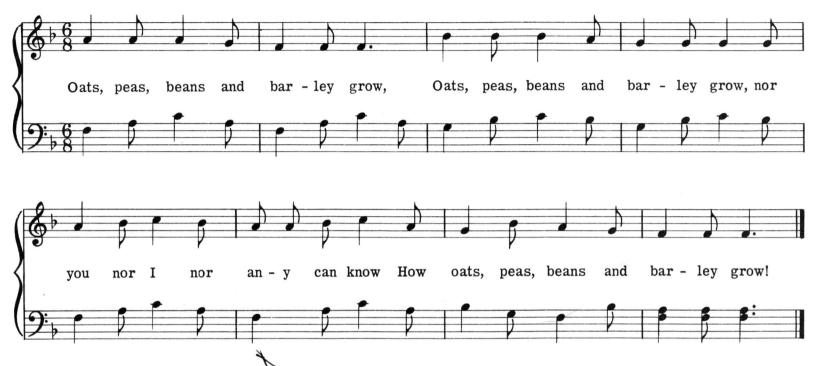

Oats, peas, beans and bar-ley grow, Oats, peas, beans and bar-ley grow, nor

you nor I nor an-y can know How oats, peas, beans and bar-ley grow!

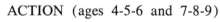

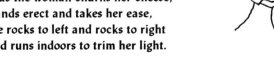

2
Thus the farmer sows his seed,
Stands erect and takes his ease.
He stamps his foot and claps his hands
And turns around to view his lands.

3
Waiting for a partner,
Waiting for a partner,
Open the ring and take her in
And then we'll gaily dance and sing.

4
Thus the woman churns her cheese,
Stands erect and takes her ease,
She rocks to left and rocks to right
And runs indoors to trim her light.

ACTION (ages 4-5-6 and 7-8-9)

All form a circle and skip to the left, singing the first stanza. As Stanza 2 begins, all the boys step forward, sowing seed as they do, and form an inner circle of boys. They act out all the parts of this stanza.

Stanza 3: Both circles skip to the left, and on the last line the girls step forward and the boys step back, so that the inner ring is now girls.

Stanza 4: The girls act out all the lines, on the last line joining the boys circle. Thus the game ends with a single circle, ready to begin again.

Sometimes that game is played with one boy as the farmer, standing in the middle. Stanza 1, the circle turns left. Stanza 2, the circle stands and the farmer acts. Stanza 3, he picks a partner while the circle again skips to the left. Stanza 4, the circle stops moving and the girl acts out the wife's part.

EENCY WEENCY SPIDER

Een - cy, ween - cy spi - der went up the wa - ter spout, Down came the rain and

washed the spi - der out, Out came the sun - shine and dried up all the

rain, and the een - cy, ween - cy spi - der went up the spout a - gain.

ACTION (ages 4-5-6)

This is an old finger play game, in which the children's creeping fingers act out the story as they sing. For example, touch index fingers to thumbs and circle them, for the first line of the song. Wriggle all fingers for the rain. Raise right hand with thumb and index finger formed into a circle for the sun.

Many years ago, when a small-sized automobile called an Austin was popular in jokes if not on the highways—long before the advent here of other small European cars—we heard children in New York singing this parody:

Eency, weency Austin went up the road to town,
Down came the rain and washed the Austin down,
Out came the sunshine and dried up all the rain,
But the eency, weency Austin was never found again.

We suspect that any group of youngsters will find it fun to make up new words and gestures to take the place of the spider.

FOX IN A BOX

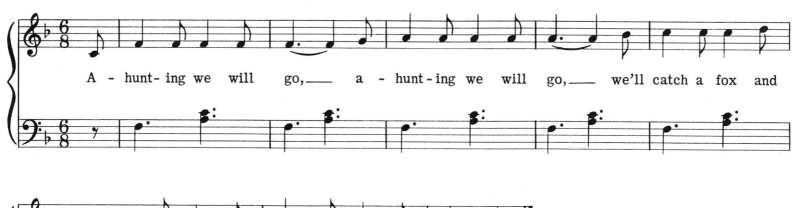

A - hunt-ing we will go,___ a - hunt-ing we will go,___ we'll catch a fox and

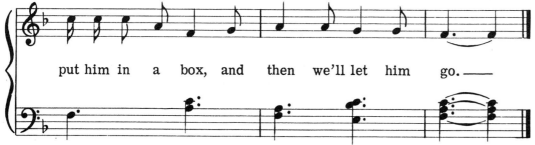

put him in a box, and then we'll let him go.___

ACTION (ages 4-5-6 and 7-8-9)

All children except one form a circle, hands joined. They skip to the left. The odd child skips in the opposite direction around the outside of the circle. At the words *we'll catch* the two children nearest the fox raise their arms and bring the arch down on the other side of him. This puts the fox inside the box. Still skipping, the children close ranks, so the fox cannot escape between them. At the word *go,* however, the children nearest the fox raise their arms and let him out.

The game starts over again at once. The fox quickly trades places with any member of the circle who now becomes a fox and skips off outside the ring, to the right.

SAN SERENI

San Se - re - ní de la bue - na, bue - na vi - da, Ha - cen a - sí, a -

sí los car - pin - ter - os, A - sí, a - sí, a - sí, a - sí me gus - ta a mi.
los za - pa - ter - os
las pro - fes - or - as
las sen - or - i - tas
los va - quer - os

ACTION I (ages 4-5-6 and 7-8-9)

This Puerto Rican singing game is universal in its design—it is a children's imitation of adult activities. All form a circle, holding hands, except for one child in the middle. They skip to the left. While singing the word *carpinteros* (carpenters), the child in the middle does a rhythmic act of sawing or hammering. For the last four measures, the children forming the circle stand still and imitate his actions.

As the song starts again, the child in the middle chooses a new actor for the next stanza, while he takes the new child's place in the ring. *Zapateros* means shoemakers; *profesoras* means teachers—lady teachers, in this form of the word; *senoritas* means teen-age girls, of course; and *vaqueros,* as your children will very well know, means cowboys. Eventually, you might add *marineros* (sailors), *médicos, chóferos* (drivers of cars), and other interesting workers.

When the children have mastered the words thoroughly, let the child in the middle sing the second line, "Hacen asi, asi los . . .," as a solo, choosing the trade himself. Children too old to play the game will still enjoy the delightful melody and an easy introduction to Spanish. A direct translation: *Saint Serení of the good, good life—they do like this, like this the carpenters—like this, like this, like this, like this it pleases me.*

ALOUETTE

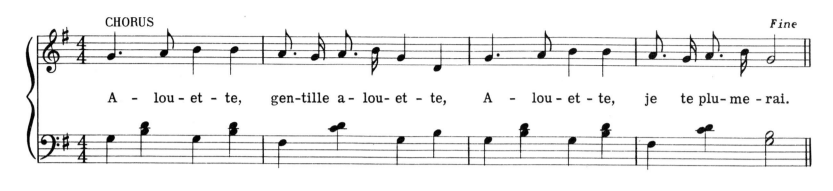

A - lou-et - te, gen-tille a- lou-et - te, A - lou-et - te, je te plu-me - rai.

Je te plu - me-rai la tête, je te plu-me-rai la tête, et la tête, et la tête.

1

Je te plu-me-rai la tête,
je te plu-me-rai la tête,
Et la tête, et la tête.

2

Je te plu-me-rai le bec,
je te plu-me-rai le bec,
Et le bec, et le bec,
et la tête, et la tête.

3

Je te plu-me-rai le nez,
je te plu-me-rai le nez,
Et le nez, et le nez,
et le bec, et le bec,
et la tête, et la tête.

4

Je te plumerai le dos.

5

Je te plumerai les pattes.

6

Je te plumerai les yeux.

7

Je te plumerai le cou.

8

Je te plumerai le queue.

ALOUETTE

ACTION (all ages)

This old favorite is a cumulative leader-and-chorus song, with accompanying hand gestures initiated by the leader and repeated by the chorus.

The first line is sung to start, repeated after each stanza, and of course at the very end. The next-to-the-last measure in the music is the cumulative part, as shown above. Thus, at the end of Stanza 8, we sing the whole list in reverse order: "Et le queue, et le queue, et le cou, et le cou, et les yeux, et les yeux," etc., down to, "et la tête, Oh!———"

The song leader, by using gestures for each part of the bird, serves two functions. He gives the singers a more active role, and he teaches the meaning of the words. Roughly translated, the song says: *Lark, dear lark, I shall pluck you. I shall pluck your head, beak, nose, back, feet, eyes, neck, and tail.*

DER KUCKUCK

Translation ESB

Auf ein - em Baum ein Kuck - uck, Sim sa -la - dim, bim ba, sa -la -
Up - on a tree a cuck - oo,

du, sa -la - dim, Auf ein - em Baum ein Kuck - uck sass.____
Up - on a tree a cuck - oo sat.____

2	2
Da kam ein junger Jägers—,	And through the woods a hunter,
Sim saladim, bim ba, saladu, saladim,	Sim saladim, bim ba, saladu, saladim,
Da kam ein junger Jägersmann.	And through the woods a hunter came.

3	3
Der schoss den armen Kuckuck,	He shot that poor old cuckoo,
Sim saladim, bim ba, saladu, saladim,	Sim saladim, bim ba, saladu, saladim,
Der schoss den armen Kuckuck todt.	He shot that poor old cuckoo dead.

4	4
Und als ein Jahr vergangen,	And after one long year had,
Sim saladim, bim ba, saladu, saladim,	Sim saladim, bim ba, saladu, saladim,
Und als ein Jahr vergangen war,	And after one long year had passed,

DER KUCKUCK

5
Da war der arme Kuckuck,
Sim saladim, bim ba, saladu, saladim,
Da war der arme Kuckuck *lebendig*!

5
We saw that poor old cuckoo,
Sim saladim, bim ba, saladu, saladim,
We saw that poor old cuckoo *alive*!

ACTION I (ages 4-5-6 and 7-8-9)

This singing game from Germany is played in a ring. Choose one child to be the cuckoo in the middle.

Stanza 1: Children hold hands and skip to the left during the first and third lines, to the right during the nonsense line. The cuckoo does whatever bird play he chooses.

Stanza 2: They hold their hands as though carrying rifles and go around the ring in an exaggerated tip-toe, singing very softly. Again, direction is reversed during the second line. The bird responds however he thinks suitable.

During the first line of Stanza 3, all face the cuckoo and slowly raise guns to firing position, just getting ready to shoot at the last syllable. During the nonsense line they immediately lower their guns and circle around, exactly as in Stanza 2. In the third line, they repeat the action of the first line, and on the word *todt* (dead) the cuckoo falls to the ground.

Stanza 4: The circle joins hands and walks, not skips, to the left, to the right, and to the left again.

Stanza 5: During the first line the circle moves slowly to the left, all the players pantomiming a search within the ring. Reverse direction for the second line. During the last line they stand still, indicating that they see the cuckoo. This stanza is sung with mock pathos. Sometimes children pantomime the wiping of eyes with imaginary handkerchiefs. On the final word, of course, the cuckoo leaps to his feet, flies merrily about for a few moments, and enters the circle.

Choose a new cuckoo and start all over.

ACTION II (all ages)

Der Kuckuck is also played as a hand game by a seated group of singers. The song leader does the actions and the singers imitate them. For the nonsense line, work out a hand and knee clapping sequence that you like and keep that unchanged for all stanzas.

Auf einem Baum—hold left forearm straight up. *Ein Kuckuck*—using right hand, thrust thumb (the bird's head) between index and middle fingers (the wings) and have the cuckoo hover above the tree. On *sass,* the bird lands on the tree.

Stanza 2: Hold hands as though carrying a rifle over the shoulder, and rise a little in seat on every other beat. This gives the group an appearance of marching.

Der schoss den armen—rifle held ready to shoot. *Kuckuck* —right hand fluttering, as before. *Todt*—the bird falls into the player's lap.

Stanza 4: Stretch arms up and out, as though awakening after a year's sleep.

Stanza 5: Hold left hand palm up, with the dead bird lying on it. On *lebendig,* have the bird fly away. An alternative for this stanza is to have the singers themselves be the cuckoo, wings held in and head drooping until the final word, at which time all jump to their feet.

MEIN HANDS

Mein hands bei mein sides, was ist das hier? Das ist mein
2. Das ist mein
3. Das ist mein

hair mop-per, mein teach-er dear. Hair mop-per, du-ven-ick-a von
sweat box-er, (etc.)
eye blink-ers,

du, Dat's what we learn in der Shul.

2
{ Sweat box-er,
{ hair mop-per,

3
{ Eye blink-ers,
{ sweat box-er,
{ hair mop-per,

4
. . . smell sniffer (nose)

5
. . . soup sipper (mouth)

88

MEIN HANDS

6	10
. . . chin chopper	. . . knee bender
7	11
. . . chest protector	. . . foot kicker
8	12
. . . bread basket (*stomach*)	. . . sit downer
9	
. . . lap sitter	

ACTION (ages 7-8-9 and 10-11-12)

This cumulative song is generally sung with a song leader who initiates gestures to accompany the words. After a few times, however, most groups will remember the words and gestures and manage perfectly well without adult help. The song was taught to us as being a Pennsylvania Dutch folk song, but we suspect that it is one of several songs that became current in the last century making good-natured fun of the language habits of those good people. We have heard the song done without the exaggerated German accent, but we think it is more amusing with it.

For the first two measures, sit up primly with hands held stiffly at sides. For the question in measures three and four, point to the hair, the forehead, the eyes, or whatever part the particular stanza refers to. Repeat this gesture for the next two measures which answer the question. For the words, *mein teacher dear,* clasp hands in front of chest, as children used to sit with hands folded on the school desk.

Measure 9 is cumulative. In the first stanza, sing *hair mopper* twice. In the ensuing stanzas you sing all the parts that have been mentioned thus far, in reverse order, once each. In the last stanza, this measure would start: "Sit downer, foot kicker, knee bender," and go through the whole list, ending up with *hair mopper* and the words of the refrain.

Some leaders use rhythm gestures for the nonsense line, *duvenicka von du,* but we prefer to return to the clasped hands position for these words and the remainder of the stanza.

In pointing out the various parts of the body, Stanza 12 requires that the singers stand up. Have them rise, point, and sit down again at measure four, again at measure six, and again at measure nine. It is always a good idea in a hand action song to include some gesture which requires broad stretching gestures or getting to one's feet. This provides a break in the subdued activity pattern and gives the big muscles a chance to work.

Even though your group will quickly outgrow the need for a song leader, they will probably enjoy taking turns in leading, themselves. This will give them an opportunity to invent different gestures and also to add more stanzas. We have seen groups of children add many, such as *brow beetlers, muscle bulgers* (the biceps), *elbow nudgers, neck tie-ers, toe dancers,* etc.

PASS THE SHOE

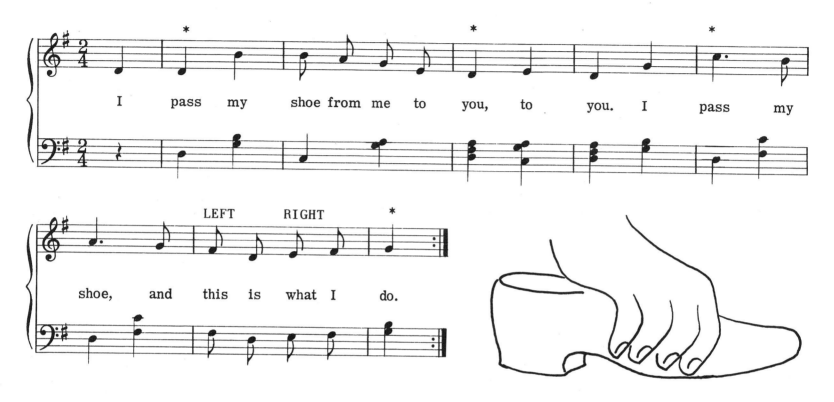

I pass my shoe from me to you, to you. I pass my

LEFT RIGHT
shoe, and this is what I do.

ACTION I (ages 10-11-12)

This simple game seems to be endlessly intriguing, and there is no upper age level.

Any number of players sit on the floor, in a circle, each having his two shoes on the floor in front of him. The song is sung quite slowly, at first, and with very precise tempo. Players pick up the two shoes in front of them, one in each hand, and pass them to the left on the down beat of measures one, three and five. Set the shoes down on the floor in front of the next person with a thump. In the seventh measure, players thump the shoes on the floor in front of the person on their left, without releasing the shoes, on the word *this;* then in front of the person on their right, on the word *what;* and finally place this same pair of shoes in front of the person on the left on

the *do* in measure eight. The song goes right on, and continues until the rhythm is firmly established and the shoes are going around without mishap. Then, gradually, start to speed it up.

Like most singing games, Pass the Shoe is cooperative rather than competitive. The player who misses is not eliminated. The problem is for the group as a whole to increase its proficiency until it can play at a rattling fast tempo.

Sometimes the game is played with a pair of shoes passed on the down beat of every measure except measure seven. We prefer it as given here, because the contrast of the fast rhythm at the end of each stanza seems to us more interesting when the tempo in the early part is twice as slow. Try it both ways, however, and see which your children prefer.

PASS THE SHOE

ACTION II (ages 7-8-9)

For children in this age range, the same game can be played with one shoe per person, instead of two each. Although the rhythm is the same, working with one hand seems to be less confusing and makes the game more fun for these youngsters.

ACTION III (ages 4-6)

The same game can be played by this age level using only one shoe for the entire group instead of one shoe per person. Pass the single shoe around the circle in the same rhythm, and have every fourth child do the left-right-pass of measures 7 and 8. Be sure that the number of children in the circle is not a multiple of 4, or the same children will always have the interesting routine at the end of the stanza. In fact, if everyone is to have a turn at this, you must have an odd number of players.

VÅRSÅNG

Fairly fast, gay

Vår - vin-dar fris-ka le - ka och hvis-ka lun-der-na om likt äls-kan-de par. Ström-mar-ne i - la,

Vore - vin-dar fris-ka leh-ka uck vis-ka lun-der-na um licked els-can-da par ström-mar - na ee - la

Slow and stately

fin - na ej hvi - la för- rän i haf-vet stört - vå-gen far. Klap-pa mitt hjär-ta, kla - ga och hör

fin - na eh vee - la för - ren ee hah-vet stört - vaw-gen far clop-pa mitt yair-ta clah- ga uck hör

Original tempo

vall-hor - nens klang bland klip-por-na dör. Ström-kar-len spe - lar, sor-ger-na de - lar va-kan kring berg och dal.

voll-hure- nens clong blond clip-por-na dör ström-car-len speh- lar, sor-yairn-na deh- lar vah-kan kring bair yuck doll.

VÅRSÅNG

NOTES ON PRONUNCIATION

The name of the song is pronounced *vore-song*. The *ö* has no English equivalent. It is the same as in German or as *eu* in French. The liquid sound of the *g* in *berg* attaches itself to the following word, as shown in the phonetics above. The *u* in *lunderna* is pronounced like a French *u,* or like the *ü* in German.

TRANSLATION

Since the words in translation make little sense to modern American ears, and since there is always an advantage to singing a folk song in its own language, we always teach and sing Vårsang in Swedish. Literally it means: "Fresh spring winds play and whisper around the grove like a loving couple. Streams hasten, to find no rest until, in the sea, they ride the breakers. My heart beats, mourns, and hears the sound of shepherd's horns dying among the cliffs. Watersprites are playing, dispersing the sorrows around hill and dale."

ACTION (ages 7-8-9 and 10-11-12)

This play party is as delightful to do—or to watch—as it is to sing. Instead of couples, it requires groups of three. Customarily each triplet has a boy flanked by girls, an ideal arrangement for a class or club in which more girls than boys are ready for a "dancey" play party. With younger children, the groups can have boys and girls in any combination. For clarity in describing the figures, we shall assume each triplet to have two girls, with one boy in the middle.

Form a large circle of triplets, as though for a promenade. Have every second triplet about face. All the triplets which turned around are now facing clockwise and will gradually move clockwise about the room. The triplets which did not about face will move counterclockwise as the play party progresses.

Each boy turns his right-hand-partner by right hands (two measures), the right hand girl of the opposite triplet by left hands (two measures), the other girl of the opposite triplet by right hands (two measures), and his own left-hand-partner by left hands (two measures). In each little group of six persons, each boy will now have circled to the right turning each of the four girls in passing.

During the four slow measures, beginners may best join hands to form circles of six, and turn two measures to the left, then two measures to the right, back to place. When the children can manage it, however, teach this figure: In each triplet, the boy joins hands with his two partners. He raises his right hand and the left hand of his right-hand-partner, making an arch. At the same time, he draws her across in front of him toward the left, and with his other hand he draws his left-hand-partner across in front of him to the right, under the arch. Drop hands as the left girl passes under. Each triplet is now again in a line, the two girls having exchanged places. The triplet joins hands in this position and bows slightly to the opposite triplet as the second measure of this section ends. Repeat in the third and fourth measures of the slow music, restoring each triplet to its original position. This figure is done slowly, with stately grace.

Measure 13: each triplet walks three little steps toward the opposite triplet, and bows slightly. Measure 14: three little steps back to place. Measures 15 and 16: triplets walk through each other, each person brushing right shoulders with the person opposite him, in passing. Each triplet now bows deeply to the new triplet facing it, with whom it will dance during the round about to begin.

JUMP ROPE JINGLES

MISS LIKE THIS
Miss, miss, pretty little miss,
And when I miss, I miss like THIS.

This jump rope rhyme does not go with the usual contest to see how long the player can continue. Here you intentionally miss on the word *this*, trying to make an amusing "blunder."

ON THE HILL
On the hill there stands a la-dy, who she is I—— do not know.
All she wants is gold and sil-ver, all she wants is a fine young man.

On   the   hill   there   stands   a   la - dy,
All   she   wants   is   gold   and   sil - ver,

who   she   is   I___   do   not   know.
all   she   wants   is   a   fine   young man.

DOUBLE DUTCH
Dutch, Dutch, double Dutch,
How much do you know? I know this much:
Ten, twenty, thirty, forty, fifty . . . .

Double Dutch is jumping over two ropes simultaneously. The rope turners turn clockwise with their right hands and counterclockwise with their left. Interestingly enough, jumping double Dutch is not as hard as it looks, but turning is a real art.

In this game players do not merely see how high they can jump on each turn. It is a continuous game. The player remembers her score when she misses, and at her next turn starts on the next multiple of ten. Set a goal in advance, and the first player to reach it wins.

HOT PEPPER
Mabel, Mabel, set the table,
Don't forget the salt and pepper!

On the word pepper the turners start to turn as fast as they can and continue until the jumper misses.

STRAWBERRY SHORTCAKE
Strawberry shortcake, cream on top,
Tell me the name of your sweetheart?
A, B, C, D, E . . .

Player jumps until she misses, and then has to tell a boy's name beginning with the last letter that she jumped. Some children play that when the jumper gets successfully through Z she must tell the name of the boy that she "really loves."

JUMP ROPE JINGLES

DUCK NAMED DICK
I had a duck and his name was Dick!
Put him in the bathtub to teach him how to swim.

Drank up all the water, ate up all the soap,
Almost died with a bubble in his throat.

Send for the doctor, send for the nurse,
Send for the lady with the alligator purse.

In came the doctor, in came the nurse,
In came the lady with the alligator purse.

"Hmph," said the doctor. "Hmph," said the nurse.
"Hmph," said the lady with the alligator purse.

"He's dead," said the doctor. "He's dead," said the nurse.
"He's dead," said the lady with the alligator purse.

In jumping to this rhyme, children act out all the stanzas except the first, using slight gestures that do not interfere with the jumping. In Stanza 2, on the words *doctor, nurse,* and *lady,* raise hand to ear, as though holding a telephone. In Stanza 3, beckon on each word *in.* The *hmph* in Stanza 4 is apparently a cough, as the jumper puts her hand over her mouth each time she says it. In the last stanza, the player wipes away imaginary tears each time she says *dead.*

HOW LONG DID THE BABY SLEEP?
Fudge, fudge, call the judge, Mama has a new-born baby!
Wrap it up in tissue paper, throw it down the escalator!
How many hours did the baby sleep?
One, two, three, four, five, six, seven . . .

Count as far as the player can go without missing—but during the counting part she must jump with her eyes tightly closed.

BUSTER BROWN
Buster Brown, touch the ground.
Buster Brown, turn around.
Buster Brown, show your shoe.
Buster Brown, will you please skidoo.

Without missing a jump the player must perform the indicated actions. After skidoo she must quickly jump out, as the chant starts again without a pause and the next girl in line must jump in on the first beat.

COUNTING RHYMES

CATCH A TIGER
Eeny, meeny, miny, mo,
Catch a tiger by the toe.
If he hollers, let him go.
Eeny, meeny, miny, mo.
Out goes Y - O - U.

IBBITY, BIBBITY
Ibbity, bibbity, sibbity, sab.
Ibbity, bibbity, canahba.
Dictionary, down the ferry,
Out goes Y - O - U!

Some people with very elegant diction pronounce the last word in the second line *canal boat,* but we and our friends stuck firmly to *canahba.*

HOT POTATO

One potato, two potato,
Three potato, four,
Five potato, six potato,
Seven potato MORE.

To count out by this rhyme, have each person hold his two clenched fists before him, forming a circle of "potatoes." Since the one who recites the rhyme uses his right hand to count with, he touches his own chin to indicate his right fist. Starting with his chin, he counts fists, in order. The fist that comes out on the word *more* is eliminated and placed behind the owner's back. When a child has had both fists disqualified, he is eliminated from the count. (When *more* comes out on the counter's chin, he merely omits it from further rounds.) The child with the last remaining fist is the winner, of course.

HOW OLD ARE YOU?

The sky is blue,
How old are you?
One, two, three, four, five, *etc.*

In this counting out rhyme, children stand in a circle with one foot extended into the ring. The counter stoops and touches feet in order, starting with his own, one foot for each count. The person whose foot is touched on the word *you* tells his age, and the counter continues around the circle saying numbers up to the age mentioned.

BOTTLE OF INK
Inka, bink, a bottle of ink,
Pull out the cork and take a drink.
Red, white, blue, black
Pour the rest down the kitchen sink.

Count on the accented syllables, four to a line.

BOUNCING RHYMES

1 - 2 - 3
One, two, three, a-lary.
I spy sister Sarie,
Sitting on a tumble-ary
Reading out of the dictionary.

Bounce the ball four times to a line. Following the fourth bounce on each line, a leg is raised and passed over the ball.

A - B - C
A, my name is *Annie* and my husband's name is *Al,*
We come from *Albany* and we sell *apricots.*

B, my name is *Betty* and my husband's name is *Ben,*
We come from *Boston* and we sell *boots.*

C, my name is *Clytemnestra* and my husband's name is *Charlemagne,*
We come from *Cochin-china* and we sell *caterpillars.*

The words in italics are variable and need only begin with the right initial letter. There are four bounces to a line, with no break in the rhythm between stanzas. Anyone who gets through Z is a full-fledged world's champion. Older children, who can play with simple words quite easily, make up stanzas like the third one given above, trying for unusual names and curious merchandise. We have often seen older children playing it without a ball, merely keeping the rhythm and aiming for unusual fill-ins and a high rate of speed.

YES, SIR! NO, SIR!
Hello, hello, hello, sir!
Meet me at the grocer.
No, sir! Why, sir?
Because I can not go, sir!

This game is for children who have graduated from 1 - 2 - 3. Here the leg goes over the ball on the third bounce of line one, the third bounce on line two, on both bounces of line three, and on the word *go* in line four.